GAME ON

GAME ON

Mastering the Art of Dating High Value Women

DARRIN ELFORD

Game On: Mastering the Art of Dating High Value Women

Copyright © 2025 by Darrin Elford

First published by Darrin Elford 2025

ISBN: 978-1-991363-51-0 (Paperback)

eISBN: 978-1-991363-52-7 (E-Book)

First edition

Acknowledgements

Writing this book has been a journey of both self-reflection and growth, and I am deeply grateful to everyone who has played a part in making it possible.

First and foremost, I want to thank the countless men who have shared their stories with me, whose struggles and triumphs have inspired many of the principles discussed in this book. Your courage to face challenges and your commitment to growth have served as a powerful reminder of the resilience and strength inherent in each of us.

I would also like to extend my heartfelt gratitude to my mentors, whose wisdom and guidance have shaped my understanding of what it truly means to be a high-value man. Their support has not only shaped the content of this book but has also played an essential role in my personal evolution.

To my family and friends—thank you for your unwavering belief in me, your encouragement, and your patience during the long hours spent writing. Your support has been invaluable, and I could not have come this far without you.

A special thanks to the editors, designers, and everyone on the team who helped bring this project to life. Your professionalism, attention to detail, and commitment to excellence have made this book what it is, and I am incredibly grateful for your dedication.

Finally, I want to thank you, the reader. You've made the decision to invest in yourself, and that alone speaks volumes about your commitment to becoming the best version of yourself. My hope is that this book has provided you with the tools, mindset, and inspiration to step into your power and create a life full of purpose, passion, and meaningful connections.

This book is just the beginning of your journey. Keep evolving, keep leading, and keep attracting everything you deserve. The best is yet to come.

Thank you.

Table of Contents

Introduction: Welcome to the Game

What this Book Is (and What it Isn't)

Let's get one thing straight from the start: **This is not a book about pickup lines, manipulation, or cheap tricks.** If you're looking for ways to "hack" your way into a woman's pants without putting in the inner work — close this book now. You won't find shortcuts here.

This book is about **transformation**. It's about becoming the kind of man who **naturally attracts** high-quality women — not because of what he says, but because of **who he is**.

It's for the guy who's tired of being overlooked, rejected, friend-zoned, or invisible… and is finally ready to face himself, get serious, and rise into his potential.

I wrote this book for the man who feels like something's missing — not just in his dating life, but in who he is. You know deep down you could be more. You could lead with confidence. You could walk into a room and be noticed without even trying. You could attract the kind of women who turn heads — not just for their looks, but for their values, intelligence, and energy.

This book is your **step-by-step guide to becoming that man**. A man of strength, discipline, confidence, and quiet power.

Now, here's what this book isn't:

- It's not about pretending to be someone you're not.

- It's not about becoming a slick "player" or chasing endless hookups.

- It's not a magic fix for your problems — it's a blueprint. You still have to do the work.

But if you're ready to be challenged, to be honest with yourself, and to build the kind of life and masculinity that women deeply respect and

desire — then keep reading. This is your call to level up. **Welcome to the game.**

Why High-Value Women Require a High-Value Man

Let's break a hard truth early on:

High-value women don't settle. They don't chase. They don't tolerate emotional chaos, weak boundaries, or inconsistent men who haven't done the work. And they sure as hell aren't impressed by surface-level charm.

Why? Because they've become women of substance.

They've invested in themselves — physically, mentally, emotionally, spiritually. They've leveled up in their careers, their health, their self-worth. They don't *need* a man to complete them… which means the only men they entertain are the ones who bring value, not drama.

And here's the key:

A high-value woman doesn't measure a man by his looks, his car, or his bank account alone. She measures him by his **presence, purpose, and power**. Not the loud, ego-driven kind of power — but the quiet confidence of a man who knows who he is, where he's going, and isn't shaken by life.

If you're not growing, you're fading in her eyes. If you're uncertain of yourself, she feels it. If you're emotionally reactive, she'll walk. If your lifestyle screams comfort, porn, bad habits, and stagnation — she'll see right through it.

The truth is, a high-value woman is a mirror. She reflects back the level of man standing in front of her. If you want to attract — and keep — a woman of value, beauty, intelligence, and strength, you've got to **become the man who can hold space for all of that**. That means sharpening your mind, leveling up your body, finding your mission, mastering your emotions, and reclaiming your masculine energy.

This book isn't just about getting dates. It's about attracting someone worth building with — and being the kind of man she'd actually *choose* to build with.

High-value women don't lower their standards. You rise to meet them — or you're replaced by someone who will. Let that sink in.

Understanding the Modern Dating Landscape

Dating today is a whole different game than it was a generation ago — and if you don't understand how the field has changed, you're already playing from behind.

Let's lay it out plainly:

Women have options. More than ever. With a few taps on her phone, a woman can connect with dozens — even hundreds — of men. And the truth is, the majority of those men are either simping, lying, or fumbling their way through interactions.

It's noisy out there. Flaky conversations. One-night stands. Games. Ghosting. Mixed signals. If you don't know who you are or what you stand for, the modern dating scene will eat you alive.

But here's where it gets interesting:

In all that chaos, there's a massive opportunity for the man who stands out. And not by being louder or more charming. But by being **clear, grounded, disciplined, and masculine** — in a world where most men are lost, reactive, and disconnected from their power.

We live in a time where a lot of men are:

- Addicted to porn and dopamine

- Lacking purpose and direction

- Emotionally weak or unavailable

- Expecting women to complete them

At the same time, women are becoming more selective, more independent, and more aware of their worth. **This creates a divide** — most men are becoming weaker, while women are raising their standards.

So what does this mean for you?

It means you can't play by old rules. You can't just "be nice" and expect results. You can't expect a woman to teach you how to be a man. **You have to bring strength, leadership, clarity, and presence to the table — or you'll keep getting overlooked, ghosted, and passed over.**

This book is about helping you thrive in this new reality. Not by complaining about it… but by outgrowing it. Because the truth is, **the modern dating world is brutal for weak men — but it opens wide for strong ones.** If you're willing to evolve, this world can be yours.

Your Transformation Starts Now

Here's the moment of truth:

You're either going to change your life… or stay exactly where you are. There's no in-between.

If you picked up this book, something inside you is already waking up. Maybe you're tired of getting ignored. Maybe you're done being the "nice guy" who finishes last. Or maybe you're just sick of living below your potential — knowing you could be more but not knowing how to get there.

Good. That pain you feel? That frustration? That's your fuel.

Because the man you are today — the one who doubts himself, hesitates, escapes into porn, parties, video games, or endless scrolling — **that man cannot attract and keep a high-value woman.**

But here's the good news:

That version of you? He's temporary. **You can outgrow him — and you will.**

This book will walk you through the exact process of transformation:

- From uncertain to confident

- From needy to grounded

- From reactive to calm and controlled

- From overlooked to unforgettable

- From chasing women to *attracting* them

But let me be clear — **no one's coming to save you**. Not me. Not a woman. Not some motivational video. **You have to save yourself.** You have to commit to doing the hard work — not just for a weekend, but for a lifestyle.

And this isn't just about dating. This is about **reclaiming your masculinity**, building a life you're proud of, and becoming the kind of man you'd respect if you met him in the mirror.

You don't need to be perfect. You just need to be in motion. Start now. Make a decision that the man you were yesterday is not the man you're going to be tomorrow. **This is your line in the sand.** Let's get to work.

The Rules Have Changed – So Must You

Let's not sugarcoat it:

The old rules don't work anymore.

Your father or grandfather might've lived in a time where being a "provider" and a decent man was enough to attract a loyal, loving woman. Back then, roles were more defined. Dating was simpler. Expectations were clearer.

But today? We're living in a hyper-connected, swipe-driven world where **attention is currency**, options are endless, and distractions are everywhere. Women don't just want a man who checks boxes — they want a man who stands out. And the truth is, **most men haven't caught up to the shift**.

They're still trying to play by outdated rules:

- "Be nice and she'll like you."

- "Wait for the right one to come along."

- "Just be yourself."

That's passive. That's weak. That's the fast track to being invisible. **The rules have changed.** Today's high-value women are powerful, educated, socially aware, and emotionally tuned in. They've done the work on themselves, and they expect you to have done the same. So if you're still sitting around hoping someone will see your "potential," or thinking the right woman will "fix" you or "complete" you — wake up.

You have to adapt. You have to evolve. You have to become the kind of man who isn't shaken by the noise — a man who leads, not follows.

And that means:

- Dropping outdated beliefs about masculinity

- Reclaiming your discipline, direction, and power

- Learning how to communicate with clarity, not confusion

- Letting go of victim energy and owning every result in your life

This book is your guide, but you're the one holding the controller. You're not here to play by the old rules anymore — **you're here to rewrite them.** So get ready. The game has changed — and now, so will you.

1

The Wake-Up Call – Facing Harsh Truths

The Clueless Male: Why You're Invisible to Women

You might think women just aren't into you. That you're not tall enough. Not rich enough. Not handsome enough. That they only go for bad boys, jerks, or guys with flashy lifestyles.

But here's the real reason you're not being seen:

You're invisible because you haven't become a man worth noticing yet.

That might sting — good. It should. Because nothing changes until you stop lying to yourself.

Let's look at what most "clueless males" are doing today:

- Living in their heads, not their bodies.

- Overthinking every move around women.

- Avoiding rejection like it's death.

- Building lives around comfort, not challenge.

- Hoping a woman will come along and give their life meaning.

And what kind of energy does that give off?

Weak. Passive. Forgettable.

High-value women aren't drawn to weakness. They're not attracted to the guy who waits for a "sign" to approach her. They're not interested in the man who seeks permission to lead or approval to speak his mind. And they definitely don't want to mother a boy pretending to be a man.

Here's the truth you need to hear:

Women don't owe you attention, affection, or attraction. You don't "deserve" anything just because you're a nice guy. Being nice is expected. What women *crave* is presence, power, certainty — the grounded energy of a man who knows who the hell he is.

The average guy today doesn't know that man. He's been shaped by comfort, not challenge. Rewarded for staying quiet, not for leading. Conditioned to suppress his masculine edge instead of sharpening it.

So what happens?

He becomes invisible. Not hated. Not rejected. Just… unnoticed. And that's the most dangerous place to be. This book is here to change that. To wake you up. To hand you the mirror. To say, "Look — this is why it's not working. Now let's fix it."

Because here's the good news:

You don't have to stay clueless. You can become the kind of man who walks into a room and shifts the energy without saying a word. But it won't come from hoping or wishing. It'll come from **doing the work.**

Ready? Let's go deeper.

The Cost of Vice, Comfort Zones and Numbing Habits

Let's be real — most men are not struggling with a lack of opportunity. They're struggling with **distraction, weakness, and avoidance**. Porn. Weed. Booze. Junk food. Video games. Social media. The modern man's diet isn't just physical — it's mental and emotional junk, too.

Here's the cold truth:

Every time you reach for a vice, you're running from something. From discomfort. From challenge. From facing your own potential.

And you can't become a high-value man if you're constantly numbing yourself to reality.

Let's break this down:

Porn:

You think it's harmless? It's not. It's robbing you of your edge, killing your drive, rewiring your brain to chase pixels instead of real women, and making you lazy in the face of rejection. You train yourself to avoid risk and expect reward without effort.

Weed & Alcohol:

If you're using it to unwind occasionally, cool. But if you're using it to escape life, silence anxiety, or avoid doing hard things — you're building a prison with velvet walls. You're trading clarity and ambition for a cheap high.

Video Games & Social Media:

Again — entertainment is fine in doses. But when you're spending hours in fantasy worlds or scrolling endless feeds, **you're not relaxing — you're escaping**. You're distracting yourself from your own mediocrity. And the worst part?

You don't even feel the damage right away. These habits don't wreck your life overnight — they just slowly, silently weaken you. They steal your time. Your focus. Your hunger. They soften your masculinity and leave you comfortable... but hollow. Meanwhile, life keeps moving. The women you want keep evolving. And you — you stay stuck. Comfortable, numbed, and confused why nothing's changing.

Here's the truth:

Comfort is killing you.

Not in an obvious way — but in a slow, corrosive way. It's the warm bath that makes you forget you're drowning. So what do you do? You **reclaim your edge**. You build habits that challenge you, not coddle you.

You train your mind, your body, your discipline — like your life depends on it. Because in a way, it does.

Every vice you give up is power you take back. And every day you choose discomfort over distraction, you move one step closer to becoming the man women respect — and desire. Time to get uncomfortable.

How Society has Softened Masculinity

Let's address the elephant in the room:

Masculinity is under attack. Not in a dramatic, victimized way — but in a quiet, cultural shift that's been happening for decades. Society doesn't celebrate strong, grounded, masculine men anymore. It tolerates them at best. Often, it mocks them. Sometimes it shames them.

We've been told masculinity is "toxic.". We've been taught that male leadership is oppressive. We've been conditioned to believe that being aggressive, dominant, or assertive is a problem — instead of what it truly is: **natural masculine energy** when rooted in discipline and purpose.

So what's the result? A generation of men afraid to be men. Soft, uncertain, hesitant, apologetic — trying to please everyone and offend no one.

We're seeing:

- Boys growing into men without strong male role models
- Fathers missing, passive, or emotionally distant
- Media pushing passive, weak male characters as "relatable"
- Schools encouraging boys to sit still, be quiet, and suppress competition
- Social pressure to prioritize being "nice" over being *real*

It's no wonder so many guys grow up confused, disconnected, and unable to lead in their own lives — let alone in a relationship.

But here's the truth you're not hearing enough:

Masculinity is not the problem.

Unconscious masculinity is. *Uncontrolled* masculinity is. Masculinity without direction, purpose, or values becomes toxic — just like anything else.

But **healthy masculinity**? It's what the world is starving for. It's focused. It's protective. It's assertive, not aggressive. It leads. It creates. It stabilizes.

And guess what?

High-value women are craving it. They don't want a man who's apologizing for his masculinity. They want a man who's embraced it, refined it, and leads with strength and integrity.

Here's the deal:

You don't need to be a caveman. You don't need to dominate or control. But you do need to reclaim your masculine core — the fire, the discipline, the direction — that makes you grounded and powerful.

Society may have softened masculinity… but you don't have to. It's time to remember who you really are — and become the man you were built to be.

Accountability: Your Life, Your Fault, Your Fix

Here's the line in the sand:

Everything in your life right now — your confidence, your results with women, your body, your bank account, your mindset — is your responsibility. Not your parents. Not your ex. Not society. Not your boss. **Yours.**

Until you fully own that truth, you will stay stuck. Most men never grow because they stay locked in a victim mindset.

They blame external things for internal problems:

- "Women only want rich guys."

- "It's harder for me because of my upbringing."

- "I just don't have the time."

- "Dating apps are rigged."

- "I don't know where to start."

Excuses feel good in the short term. They take the pressure off. But **every excuse is a brick in the wall between you and the man you could be.**

Here's what high-value men understand:

- If you're out of shape — that's on you.

- If your dating life sucks — that's on you.

- If you have no purpose or plan — that's on you.

- If women don't respect you — that's on you.

The good news? If it's your fault... it's also **your fix**. That means you're not powerless. You're not broken. You're simply untrained. Undisciplined. Unfocused. **And all of that can change — the moment you stop outsourcing responsibility.** This is where everything starts to shift.

When you say:

"I created this version of me — and now I'm going to create something better." No more blaming. No more waiting. No more hoping someone else will come along and save you. You don't need saving. You need to **step up**, take the hit, and do what's required to evolve.

Every chapter of this book is built on this foundation. If you won't own your life, your results, and your future — **nothing else in here will work.** So decide, right now:

You are the problem. You are the solution. You are the point of change.

No one's coming. It's on you — and that's the most powerful truth you'll ever accept.

Setting Your Vision: What Kind of Man Will You Become?

It's time to ask yourself a powerful question: What kind of man do you want to be?

No, seriously. Stop and think about it. Do you want to be the guy who's always on the sidelines, watching life pass by? The guy who *hopes* things change but never puts in the effort? The guy who shows up for women, but doesn't show up for himself? Or do you want to be the kind of man who commands respect, who's unstoppable in his own life, and who has women looking at him not just for what he *does*, but for who he *is*?

You need to create a vision for the man you want to become — and it needs to be crystal clear. No more vague ideas like "I want to be successful" or "I want to get my life together." That's not a vision. That's a wish.

A strong vision is something you can see, feel, and aim for every single day. It's a blueprint for your future, a mental image of the *best* version of yourself — and you have to hold that image in your mind, even when things get tough.

Ask yourself:

- What does this man look like when he wakes up? What does he do first thing in the morning?

- What kind of habits does he have? How does he take care of his body, his mind, his soul?

- How does he dress? How does he carry himself?

- What does his career look like? How does he lead in his work and personal life?

- What does he stand for? What values guide him?

- What does his social circle look like? Who does he spend time with?

- How does he talk to women? How does he approach them? How does he attract and keep the attention of high-value women?

Your vision isn't some far-off fantasy. It's who you are becoming, right now. You need to visualize this version of yourself in detail. Then, you need to ask yourself: What would that man do today?

What does he do to make his body strong? What does he do to improve his mental toughness? What does he do to level up his finances, his mindset, his relationships?

Every decision, every action, needs to align with this vision. The man you want to be is not a distant ideal — he's the person you *become* with each choice you make. The more clearly you see him, the more power you have to step into his shoes every day.

Here's the thing:

This vision isn't a dream. It's a mission. And when you have a mission, when you're driven by a clear sense of purpose, nothing can stop you. Not distractions. Not doubts. Not challenges. Because you know exactly who you're becoming and why it matters.

So, now that you've asked yourself the hard question — what kind of man will you become? The answer starts now. The path is yours to take. And the vision? It's waiting for you to step into it.

2

Destroying the Old Self – Breaking Bad Habits

Identifying the Patterns that Sabotage You

Here's the hard truth: **Your life is the sum of your habits.** And if you're stuck in the same patterns — self-doubt, procrastination, distraction, comfort-seeking behaviors — you're keeping yourself from stepping into your true potential.

But here's the catch:

Most of these sabotaging patterns are invisible.

They've become so ingrained in your daily routine that you don't even notice them anymore. They're like the background noise of your life, always there, quietly dictating your actions and reactions. But you have to see them clearly if you ever want to break free.

The first step in destroying your old self is identifying the patterns that are holding you back.

Start by looking at the areas where you're failing or stuck:

- **Your dating life**: Are you constantly attracting women who aren't a good match for you? Are you getting rejected, ghosted, or just not taking action when you need to?

- **Your career and finances**: Are you stagnant in your job? Are you always talking about what you "could" do but never taking the steps to make it happen?

- **Your body**: Do you keep making excuses about why you're out of shape, unhealthy, or unmotivated to improve?

- **Your mindset**: Do you constantly tell yourself you'll never be enough or that you're not cut out for success?

Now, let's dig deeper into the patterns that could be driving these issues:

1. The Comfort Trap: Seeking Instant Gratification

You might be addicted to comfort — the quick dopamine hit that comes from escaping into distractions like TV, social media, video games, junk food, or substances. The pattern is simple: **Avoid discomfort at all costs**. But here's the problem: comfort is the enemy of growth. The more you avoid discomfort, the more you shrink from real challenges — and the more you procrastinate on the things that truly matter in life, like building your confidence, improving your health, or pursuing your goals.

2. Procrastination and Inaction: Waiting for the Right Moment

If you're constantly waiting for the "right time" to make a move, whether it's approaching women, starting a business, or getting fit, you're stuck in a pattern of inaction.

The truth is, **the right time will never come.** You'll always find an excuse to delay, whether it's fear of failure, self-doubt, or the idea that you're "not ready yet."

This habit is toxic because it keeps you from ever making progress. If you're waiting for the perfect moment to start — whether it's with women, your fitness, or your career — **you'll be waiting forever.**

3. People-Pleasing: Seeking Validation from Others

If you're constantly bending over backward to please others — especially women — then you're reinforcing the pattern of **seeking external validation**. This behavior stems from a lack of self-worth and a deep fear of rejection.

You become the man who puts others' needs before your own, sacrificing your time, energy, and desires to get approval. And guess what? **Women can sense this weakness a mile away.** When you're always putting her needs first, you're not showing up as the confident, masculine man she wants. Instead, you're showing her that your value depends on her approval.

4. Fear of Rejection: Playing it Safe

Another dangerous pattern is the fear of rejection. If you let this fear dictate your actions, you'll stay on the sidelines of life, never taking risks, never putting yourself out there.

When it comes to women, this pattern manifests as avoiding making the first move, overthinking everything, or staying passive in your approach. You're afraid of being turned down, so you stay in your head instead of in the game. But here's the harsh reality: **you can't win if you don't play**.

Rejection isn't the end of the world. It's simply part of the process. The more you embrace it and push through the fear, the more you'll grow. **But as long as you stay afraid of it, you'll keep holding yourself back.**

5. Negative Self-Talk: Believing You're Not Enough

Your internal dialogue is more powerful than you think. If you've been telling yourself that you're "not good enough," "not attractive enough," or "not capable enough," then you've built a pattern of negative self-talk that's crippling your confidence.

Your brain believes what you tell it — so if you constantly reinforce the idea that you're inadequate, your actions will reflect that belief. Women can sense low self-esteem, and so can everyone else. If you don't believe in your own value, no one else will either.

6. Emotional Reactivity: Letting Feelings Control You

Emotional reactivity is when you let your feelings — especially negative ones — dictate your actions. Whether it's anger, frustration, sadness, or fear, you allow these emotions to drive you rather than staying calm and controlled. When you're emotionally reactive, you lack the self-control that makes a man truly attractive. High-value women want a man who is emotionally grounded, not one who gets triggered easily or throws temper tantrums when things don't go his way.

Being emotionally reactive only causes chaos and confusion in your life and relationships. The more you let your emotions control you, the less control you have over your own life.

The Bottom Line:

You need to **identify the patterns that are sabotaging you** before you can change them. These habits didn't form overnight — and they won't disappear without deliberate effort and awareness. But once you spot them, you can begin the work of dismantling them and replacing them with new, empowering habits.

Start by getting brutally honest with yourself. Look at your life objectively, and ask:

- What do I keep doing that's not serving me?

- What am I hiding from?

- Where am I letting fear, distraction, or comfort rule my decisions?

- What do I need to let go of to move forward?

Remember: **Awareness is the first step to transformation**. Once you see these patterns, you can break them, and that's when real change begins.

Addiction, Porn and Escapism: Cutting the Chains

Let's talk about something uncomfortable — but absolutely necessary. **If you're addicted to porn, substances, or any other form of escapism, you're sabotaging your potential.**

These distractions aren't just harmless indulgences. They're chains that bind you to a version of yourself that's weak, passive, and disconnected from reality. But here's the truth: **You're in control**. These chains can be broken, but it starts with acknowledging their power over you and making a choice to step into freedom.

The Porn Trap: Escaping Reality, Destroying Your Masculinity

It's not just a "guy thing." Porn isn't just about seeking pleasure — it's an addiction that rewires your brain, makes you numb to real connection, and drains your sexual energy.

When you spend hours watching pixels on a screen, you're training your mind to expect *instant gratification* and *fantasy* rather than real-life challenge and engagement.

Here's the problem with porn:

- **It numbs you**. Every time you indulge, you train yourself to avoid the discomfort of real life. You stop having the drive to approach women, you lose the edge that makes you attractive, and you start treating real intimacy as a distant, unrealistic fantasy.

- **It damages your self-control**. Every time you give in to the urge, you reinforce the habit of avoiding discomfort. That means you avoid doing the work that'll get you ahead in life — whether it's your fitness, your career, or building meaningful relationships.

- **It destroys your sexual health**. What starts as curiosity or boredom quickly becomes a crutch. Over time, porn weakens your libido, reduces your drive, and distorts your perception of women. Instead of seeing women as complex, beautiful individuals, you start objectifying them, unable to connect on a deeper level.

You're training your mind to be weak. And that's exactly why it's so important to **cut the chains**.

Substances & Escapism: Temporary Relief, Permanent Damage

Substances — whether it's weed, alcohol, or anything else — often come with the promise of temporary relief. They dull the pain, make you forget your worries, and put you in a state where you can "relax" and forget about the challenges of life.

But here's the reality:

Every time you lean on substances to cope, you rob yourself of growth. You delay your ability to handle real stress, face your fears, and build the mental resilience required to live at a higher level.

The True Cost of Escapism:

- **Emotional avoidance**: Instead of dealing with the discomfort of emotions, you numb them with substances, porn, or distractions. This keeps you from truly processing and growing.

- **Passivity**: Escapism keeps you in a passive state, avoiding responsibility for your life. You're not pushing forward or solving problems. You're just avoiding them.

- **Disconnection from your true self**: Every time you escape, you disconnect from your authentic, powerful self. You stop living consciously and start living reactively.

When you're constantly running from your problems, you become weaker. You stay stuck in a cycle of "escape and numb" instead of facing reality and taking control of it.

Cutting the Chains: The Road to Freedom

Here's the good news: **You can break free.** It won't be easy. It won't be quick. But it's possible — and it's worth every ounce of effort. The first step? **Admit you're chained**.

Admit that porn, substances, or escapism have control over you. Recognizing the power they have over your life is the first step in taking your power back.

Next? **Replace the escape with something real.**

Instead of running to a screen or substance for comfort, replace it with something that will actually make you better. Hit the gym. Read a book that challenges you. Invest in learning a new skill. Do the work that will improve your life, not delay it.

Then, **build resilience**. You have to face discomfort, not avoid it. The more you challenge yourself in the real world, the stronger you'll become mentally, emotionally, and physically. It will feel uncomfortable at first, but it's through this discomfort that you'll grow into the man you're capable of becoming.

The Power of Self-Control

Breaking free from addiction and escapism requires **self-control**. But here's the truth: **Self-control is like a muscle** — the more you use it, the stronger it becomes. You don't need to be perfect, but you do need to be **consistent**.

Every time you resist the urge to escape, you build your inner strength. Every time you choose real growth over momentary pleasure, you align yourself with your higher purpose.

And eventually? **The chains break**. You start living on your own terms. You reclaim your masculinity. You feel confident, powerful, and in control of your own life. This isn't an easy process, but it is a necessary one. **Cut the chains** of addiction and escapism and start living the life you were meant to live.

Discomfort is the Catalyst for Change

If you want to transform your life and attract the kind of women who are high-value, you must first understand this fundamental truth: *discomfort is the catalyst for change*. You will not grow by staying in your comfort zone. In fact, the greatest shifts in your life will come from pushing against the resistance of what feels familiar.

We all have a tendency to stick with what we know because it feels safe. But safety doesn't breed growth. Safety breeds stagnation. As long as you're comfortable, you're not challenging yourself to evolve. And in the dating game—especially when you're aiming to attract high-value women—stagnation is your worst enemy.

The women you want to attract aren't interested in a man who has nothing to offer but the same old routine, the same habits, the same mindset. They are looking for someone who is willing to take risks, someone who is driven, someone who grows, and—most importantly—someone who understands that change requires discomfort.

The Fear of Change

The first obstacle you will encounter is fear. Fear of failure. Fear of rejection. Fear of making a fool of yourself. But here's the thing: fear is often a sign that you're on the verge of something great.

Consider this: every successful man you admire, whether in business, in relationships, or in life, has walked through the valley of discomfort. Whether they're going through the struggle of personal reinvention, dealing with the fallout of bad decisions, or simply fighting the urge to stay in the comfort zone of mediocrity, they've learned that discomfort is the prerequisite for true success.

When you face discomfort, your brain is essentially signaling that something important is happening. You're on the cusp of growth. Embrace it. Lean into it. Because the more you resist, the more you delay your own transformation.

Breaking Old Habits

If you want to date high-value women, you must understand the habits that are holding you back. You need to destroy the old self—the version of you that hides behind bad habits, toxic beliefs, and self-sabotaging behaviors. Every time you give into old patterns, you're reinforcing a version of yourself that isn't in alignment with the man you need to be to attract high-value women.

The most common bad habits? Procrastination, fear of rejection, the tendency to play games, being too passive, or the opposite: being overly aggressive in an attempt to overcompensate. These are the crutches you've leaned on, and now it's time to put them down.

Let's be real: *change is hard*. But it's not impossible. You don't need to change overnight, but you do need to start small. Challenge the excuses you've made for your behavior. If you're scared of rejection, put yourself out there anyway. If you tend to avoid hard conversations, confront them head-on.

Every time you do something that feels uncomfortable, you chip away at the old self. Every step outside your comfort zone is a victory. And in that process, you're not just transforming your habits; you're transforming your identity.

Embrace the Growth Zone

In the discomfort zone, you'll experience fear. But if you persist long enough, you will break through to the growth zone. This is where the magic happens.

Growth doesn't come from being stagnant. It doesn't come from waiting for the "right time." It doesn't come from comfort. It comes from being willing to feel the discomfort of stretching yourself, of risking failure, and of daring to be better than you were yesterday.

When you make that shift, you not only open up new possibilities in your dating life, but you also create a foundation for long-term personal success. High-value women are not impressed by empty words or promises—they are drawn to men who embody what they preach. The most powerful version of yourself will always be the one who understands that discomfort is not a barrier, but the doorway to your next level.

So the question is: are you ready to step through that door?

Discipline Over Motivation

In the world of dating high-value women, and frankly, in any area of life, there is a myth that motivation is the key to success. We often hear people say, "Just stay motivated," or "Find what inspires you," as if that alone will propel you forward. But here's the truth: *motivation is fleeting*. It's a burst of energy that can get you started, but it won't sustain you. *Discipline*, however, is the secret weapon that will see you through the grind and lead you to long-term success.

When it comes to transforming yourself—whether it's breaking bad habits or building the kind of confidence and self-assurance that attracts high-value women—motivation will only carry you so far. In fact, relying on motivation alone is one of the most dangerous things you can do because it sets you up for inconsistency and failure. Motivation is like a spark. It might light the fire, but discipline is the fuel that keeps it burning.

The Illusion of Motivation

Let's be honest. Some days, you're going to wake up feeling like you can conquer the world. You'll feel motivated, driven, ready to take on new challenges and push yourself in ways you've never done before. But then there are the other days—the days when your energy is low, when you feel tired, distracted, or even just plain lazy.

This is the harsh reality: motivation doesn't work on the days you don't feel like it. If you're relying on motivation to get things done, you're setting yourself up for inconsistency. Motivation is a fleeting emotion, a temporary high that fades when life gets tough. When you have a goal of attracting high-value women, you can't afford to be inconsistent.

The Power of Discipline

Discipline, on the other hand, is a muscle you can build over time. It's the act of doing what needs to be done, whether you feel like it or not. It's about showing up even when you're not motivated. It's about staying consistent in your actions, your efforts, and your mindset, no matter what obstacles you face. And, unlike motivation, discipline doesn't disappear when the going gets tough—it gets stronger.

When you focus on discipline, you shift from depending on temporary bursts of energy to creating sustainable habits that lead to real, lasting results. Whether it's staying committed to your fitness routine, improving your social skills, or continually working on self-improvement, discipline turns actions into automatic behaviors that don't require motivation to get started.

Building Discipline in Dating

So how do you apply discipline to your dating life? Let's break it down.

1. **Consistent Self-Improvement**: To attract high-value women, you need to continuously grow as a person. This means setting aside time every day to improve your mindset, physical health, and social skills. Discipline ensures you put in the work even when you're not feeling inspired. Whether it's reading, going to the gym, or practicing your communication skills, consistent effort is the key to success.

2. **Pushing Past Rejection**: Rejection is part of the game, and it can be hard to keep putting yourself out there. But with discipline, you'll bounce back faster and keep trying. Instead of letting rejection defeat you, you'll use it as motivation to refine your approach and keep moving forward.

3. **Building Confidence**: Confidence isn't something you either have or don't have; it's something you build through disciplined action. Every time you put yourself in a situation where you have to take risks—whether it's starting a conversation with a woman or taking the lead on a date—you're building the muscle of confidence. It's not about waiting for confidence to magically appear; it's about practicing it consistently.

4. **Staying True to Your Values**: It's easy to be swayed by temporary feelings or external validation, but true discipline lies in sticking to your core values and vision. The discipline to stay true to who you are, to never settle for less than you deserve, and to prioritize your own growth and self-worth over momentary gratification is what will make you stand out to high-value women.

Motivation vs. Discipline in Action

Here's an example: imagine you've just met someone you're really attracted to. The spark of motivation is there—you feel the butterflies, the excitement. But the first few interactions don't go as smoothly as you hoped. Maybe she's not as responsive as you imagined, or maybe you feel unsure of what to say next. If you rely on motivation to push you forward, it's easy to let self-doubt creep in and back off.

Discipline, however, tells you to stick to your plan. It reminds you that personal growth isn't linear and that setbacks are part of the process. It encourages you to push through the discomfort, learn from the experience, and continue your pursuit with even more wisdom.

Discipline doesn't wait for motivation—it makes its own.

The End Result

In the end, relying on discipline over motivation creates a consistent, strong version of yourself that high-value women will naturally gravitate towards. It's not about a one-time burst of effort. It's about creating a lifestyle of consistent, deliberate action that aligns with your goals. Whether it's improving your dating life or building a fulfilling career, discipline is the unshakable foundation you need to succeed.

You will have days when motivation is nowhere to be found. But when discipline is your driving force, you'll keep showing up, doing the work, and steadily moving towards the man you want to become—and the women you want to attract.

Designing a New Daily Operating System

If you want to attract high-value women, you need more than just a change in mindset or a few improved habits here and there. You need a *system*. A daily operating system that runs your life with precision, purpose, and power. This is where the magic happens—when you design a routine that aligns with your highest goals and values, transforming your potential into real-world success.

The truth is, most people float through life with no clear structure. They react to the demands of the day without any clear direction or strategy. And this is where they get stuck. When it comes to mastering dating, relationships, and building the kind of life that attracts the caliber of women you desire, success doesn't come from randomness. It comes from a carefully designed, intentional, and disciplined daily routine. The kind of system that works for you—not the other way around.

Why a Daily Operating System is Crucial

The world's most successful people, whether in business, fitness, or dating, don't get there by accident. They've designed their lives with intention. Your daily operating system determines how efficiently you execute the tasks that matter, how much time you dedicate to self-improvement, and how you prioritize the things that will get you closer to your goals.

For dating high-value women, a solid operating system ensures that you show up as the best version of yourself every single day, consistently moving closer to your ideal lifestyle and personal growth. Without a clear system, you risk drifting through life, reacting to external forces instead of proactively shaping your future.

The Components of Your New Daily Operating System

So how do you design a daily operating system that supports your transformation? Let's break it down into key components that you can easily incorporate into your day-to-day life.

1. Morning Rituals: Start Strong

The way you start your day sets the tone for everything that follows. High performers know that the first few hours of your day are crucial in determining how much you get done and the quality of your energy. This is your time to invest in yourself.

- Wake Up Early: Successful people wake up early because it gives them the advantage of starting the day before the distractions of the world take over. Waking up at least 30-60 minutes before the rest of the world ensures you have time to center yourself and get focused.

- Morning Movement: Whether it's a workout, stretching, or a short jog, getting your body moving in the morning wakes you up and boosts your energy levels. Exercise not only strengthens your physical body but also builds mental resilience—something that will translate into your dating life.

- Mindset Work: Spend at least 10-15 minutes in focused thought. This could be meditation, affirmations, journaling, or visualization. Set the intention for the day and visualize yourself as the confident, high-value man you are becoming. This prepares your mind for success and puts you in a positive, proactive mindset.

2. Goal Setting and Planning: Structure Your Day

A day without a clear plan is a day wasted. One of the most powerful parts of your operating system is your ability to organize your day around the most important tasks that drive you toward your goals.

- Set Clear, Specific Goals: What do you want to achieve today, and how does that contribute to your bigger goals? If you want to attract high-value women, make sure your goals include things like improving your social confidence, making meaningful connections, and refining your physical appearance. Break down these larger goals into specific tasks that can be completed in a single day.

- Time Block Your Day: Time blocking is the practice of dedicating specific blocks of time to specific tasks. Whether it's work, personal development, socializing, or even downtime, time blocking keeps you on track and focused. The key here is intentionality—don't let distractions derail you.

- Prioritize High-Value Activities: Ask yourself: *What are the most impactful actions I can take today?* This could include setting up dates, having deep conversations with women, or working on your career. Don't let the smaller, less important tasks steal your time and energy.

3. Work and Productivity: Be Relentless in Pursuit of Your Goals

Your daily operating system needs to include a system for getting things done. High-value women are attracted to men who are productive, disciplined, and ambitious—not to those who waste time or lack direction. Your ability to execute will set you apart.

- Focus on Results, Not Effort: It's not about working harder—it's about working smarter. You want to design a system that helps you achieve the outcomes you desire with the least amount of wasted effort. Create measurable, actionable steps for every project and use tools or habits that allow you to focus deeply on high-priority tasks.

- Embrace the 80/20 Rule: The Pareto Principle tells us that 20% of your activities will yield 80% of your results. Identify which 20% of tasks are most valuable to your success in dating and life, and prioritize them every day. Is it improving your physical health? Is it honing your social skills? Whatever it is, do it consistently.

4. Evening Reflection and Wind-Down: Close the Day with Intention

Your evening routine is just as important as your morning. How you end your day will influence how well you sleep, how rested you feel, and how much you accomplish the following day.

- Review Your Day: Take 10-15 minutes each evening to reflect on your day. What went well? What could you have done better? This reflection time helps you stay aligned with your goals and refine your daily system.

- Practice Gratitude: Being grateful for what you have—and recognizing your daily successes—will keep your mindset positive and prevent feelings of frustration or burnout. Write down at least three things you're grateful for each night.

- Wind-Down Routine: A solid wind-down routine signals to your brain that it's time to sleep. Limit screen time, avoid stimulants, and create a calming environment with books, relaxation, or meditation.

Make It Custom

Remember, this daily operating system is *yours*. There's no one-size-fits-all approach. The system you design should be tailored to your unique goals, rhythm, and lifestyle. Experiment with different habits and routines until you find the combination that works best for you.

But the key is consistency. When you have a well-oiled daily routine that supports your goals and embodies the discipline needed to show up as the best version of yourself, attracting high-value women becomes the natural result.

Your new daily operating system is more than just a structure—it's the roadmap to becoming the man you were always meant to be. So start designing it now, and let your new system do the heavy lifting.

3

The Inner Game – Building Confidence from the Core

Self-Worth vs. Self-Esteem: Know the Difference

When it comes to building unshakable confidence and attracting high-value women, understanding the difference between *self-worth* and *self-esteem* is critical. They may sound similar, and most people use them interchangeably, but they represent two distinct concepts that play unique roles in shaping how you perceive yourself and how others perceive you.

In the pursuit of mastering your inner game, *self-worth* and *self-esteem* are the foundation of the confident, grounded man you need to become. And the better you understand how they differ—and how they work together—the stronger your internal framework will be. This knowledge doesn't just enhance your confidence; it aligns you with the qualities that high-value women look for in a partner.

Self-Worth: The Core of Who You Are

Self-worth is your inherent value as a human being—*the belief that you are valuable and deserving of love, respect, and success simply because you exist*. It's a fundamental understanding that doesn't fluctuate based on external circumstances, achievements, or other people's opinions. It's not something you *earn* or something that can be taken away—it's a core truth that you must embrace and internalize.

Your self-worth is rooted deep inside you, in the very essence of who you are. It's about accepting yourself, flaws and all, without needing external validation to feel good about yourself. This is why self-worth is so powerful—it's unshakable, constant, and independent of external outcomes.

When your self-worth is high, you stop seeking approval from others. You no longer chase validation through achievements or the approval of others, and you stop measuring your value by external standards. You can walk into a room, meet a woman, and know that you are worthy of her time, attention, and respect— without needing to prove it.

The Key to Self-Worth:

Self-worth is about unconditional acceptance of yourself. It's understanding that, regardless of your achievements or shortcomings, you are a person of value, deserving of love and respect.

Self-Esteem: The Reflection of Your Achievements

While self-worth is the core, self-esteem is the outward reflection of it. Self-esteem is shaped by your accomplishments, experiences, and the way you relate to the world around you. It's the feeling of confidence and pride that you gain when you achieve something or when you live in alignment with your values.

Self-esteem fluctuates—it can rise when you're performing well and feel successful, but it can also dip when you encounter setbacks, face rejection, or make mistakes. It's more fluid and tied to the external world, whereas self-worth is constant. Self-esteem is earned, built over time, and often influenced by your ability to meet the expectations you've set for yourself.

Think of self-esteem as the mirror in which you see yourself reflected based on your actions. If you're consistently doing the work to build your physical health, pursuing your passions, and making progress toward your goals, your self-esteem will rise. But if you're neglecting your growth or not meeting your own standards, your self-esteem will suffer.

The Key to Self-Esteem:

Self-esteem is about how you perceive your value based on your actions and results. It's linked to your achievements, the way you show up in the world, and how well you align your behavior with your personal values.

Why You Need Both

Now, why is it so important to distinguish between the two? Because the foundation of true confidence lies in building a strong sense of *self-worth* while simultaneously working to improve your *self-esteem*. Let's break it down:

- **Self-Worth as the Anchor**: If you anchor your sense of value in self-worth, it means that no matter what happens—whether you succeed or fail, whether a date goes well or falls flat—you know your worth is intrinsic and unchanging. You are not defined by external events or judgments. High-value women are naturally drawn to men who know their worth, because it signals confidence and emotional stability. They want someone who isn't swayed by every external success or failure.

- **Self-Esteem as the Boost**: Self-esteem, on the other hand, gives you the confidence to take action and pursue your goals. When your self-esteem is high, you take pride in your achievements, push yourself to be better, and take risks with the knowledge that you're capable of handling challenges. Women are drawn to men who have high self-esteem because they radiate competence and strength. When you're actively working to increase your self-esteem—through self-improvement, success, and learning—you become more attractive to others.

The magic happens when your self-worth is rooted in the certainty of who you are, while your self-esteem grows through intentional action and success. When both are aligned, your confidence becomes a natural, magnetic force.

Balancing Self-Worth and Self-Esteem

The key to building long-lasting confidence—and ultimately attracting the high-value women you desire—is to nurture both your self-worth and self-esteem.

1. **Start with Self-Worth**: Build your self-worth by learning to love and accept yourself unconditionally. Practice self-compassion. Recognize that you don't have to be perfect to be worthy of love and respect. If you struggle with this, start by identifying your positive qualities and reminding yourself that you are deserving, just as you are.

2. **Work on Building Self-Esteem**: Your self-esteem will naturally rise as you work on your goals and take positive actions in your life. Set and achieve small goals, push yourself to grow, and take pride in your progress. It's important to recognize that failures or setbacks don't diminish your worth; they are simply opportunities for growth.

3. **Don't Rely on External Validation**: While high self-esteem can be impacted by external factors like success or social feedback, high self-worth keeps you grounded. You don't need anyone's validation to know you're valuable. When you stop seeking external validation, you reclaim your power and stop feeling desperate for approval.

Conclusion: The Ultimate Confidence Formula

To truly master your inner game, you must come to understand the difference between self-worth and self-esteem. Your *self-worth* is unshakeable and does not depend on the whims of external success, while your *self-esteem* grows as a result of your actions and achievements.

High-value women are drawn to men who are grounded in their worth and who exhibit confidence based on their real accomplishments. By strengthening both aspects of yourself, you build the foundation for lasting confidence. So, know your worth, build your esteem, and step into the world with the kind of unshakable confidence that attracts the high-value women you deserve.

The Masculine Mindset Shift: You are the Prize

One of the most transformative mindset shifts you must make to succeed in dating—and in life—is this: *you are the prize*. Not in an arrogant, egotistical, or self-absorbed way, but from a place of deep self-respect, self-awareness, and masculine certainty.

Most men operate from a place of scarcity when it comes to women. They chase. They over-invest. They pedestalize. They believe the woman is the prize, and they act accordingly—bending over backwards to win her approval, often at the cost of their own self-respect. And that's exactly why they lose. High-value women don't respond to neediness. They respond to strength.

To master the inner game and become the kind of man who effortlessly attracts high-value women, you must flip the script. You must operate from a *masculine mindset of abundance, purpose, and self-worth*. You must understand, on a visceral level, that *you bring something valuable to the table*—and any woman who comes into your life is *joining* your mission, not becoming the mission.

The Trap of the Validation Seeker

When you believe a woman is the prize, your behavior becomes reactive. You subconsciously put her on a pedestal. You try too hard. You overthink your texts, your appearance, your words. You start tailoring your personality to what you think she wants, instead of being grounded in who you truly are.

This behavior screams *lack*. It communicates to her that you believe she is above you—that her attention, her affection, her presence is more valuable than yours. And nothing kills attraction faster than a man who puts himself beneath her just to gain favor.

High-value women are not attracted to men who chase validation. They are attracted to men who *radiate value*. Men who are selective, composed, and centered. Men who have the confidence to walk away—not out of bitterness, but because they know their worth.

What It Really Means to Be the Prize

Being the prize doesn't mean you walk around with inflated confidence or act like you're better than everyone else. It means you are a man of *substance*—a man who lives with purpose, has standards, and values his time, energy, and presence.

You are the prize because:

- You've done the work on yourself—physically, mentally, emotionally.

- You live a purpose-driven life. You don't chase women; you lead yourself toward a greater mission.

- You are emotionally grounded. You don't need constant reassurance or attention to feel secure.

- You have options, but you're selective. You don't settle, and you don't chase.

- You know how to give value—but only to those who are worthy of receiving it.

When you embrace this mindset, something powerful happens: *you stop acting from desperation and start operating from strength*. You're no longer trying to convince women of your worth. Instead, you calmly let them discover it.

Masculine Energy Attracts Feminine Energy

At the core of this shift is a return to your masculine essence. Masculine energy is about leadership, direction, and grounded confidence. It doesn't seek approval—it *commands* respect simply by how it shows up. When you embody the mindset that you are the prize, you naturally attract feminine energy—women who are confident in themselves but also deeply drawn to strong masculine presence.

Remember: feminine energy is pulled toward stability, certainty, and confidence. Not performance. Not games. Not empty bravado. When you step fully into your masculine frame and believe you are the prize, you create the dynamic that high-value women find irresistible.

Practical Ways to Embody the "I Am the Prize" Mindset

Here's how to anchor this mindset into your daily life:

1. **Raise Your Standards** – Stop entertaining low-effort women or relationships that don't serve you. If you're the prize, not everyone gets access. You don't settle. You qualify women for your life just as much as they're qualifying you.

2. **Lead Your Life First** – Before you focus on dating, get locked in on your goals. Your fitness, career, purpose, and discipline are not optional—they're foundational. When you lead your life with conviction, you become naturally attractive.

3. **Be Willing to Walk Away** – The prize never clings. The man who values himself never fears loss, because he knows what he brings to the table. If a woman isn't aligned with your values or vision, let her go with grace and strength.

4. **Don't Chase, Invite** – You're not here to impress. You're here to express. Lead with authenticity and confidence, and let women *choose* to be part of your life. You don't chase the spotlight—you *are* the spotlight.

5. **Control Your Frame** – Your frame is your mental and emotional state. Guard it. Don't let a woman's mood, approval, or beauty pull you out of alignment. Stay centered. That's how a man who is the prize holds power in any interaction.

Final Word: Step Into Your Throne

Becoming the man who attracts high-value women starts when you stop looking for something outside yourself to complete you. You are not chasing women—you are building a kingdom. And the woman who enters your life is not your purpose—she is your complement.

You are the prize because you live with purpose, value yourself, and lead with intention. When you truly believe that—and back it up with action—you become the man she *wants*, not the man who's trying to prove he's worth wanting.

So step into your throne. You're not here to chase. You're here to choose.

Eliminating Neediness and Desperation

If there's one energy that repels high-value women faster than anything else, it's *neediness*. Desperation is the death of attraction. It's the unspoken energy that says, *"I need you to like me so I can feel good about myself."* And let me be clear: no matter how well-dressed you are, how smooth your words, or how many boxes you check on paper—if you're radiating neediness, it *will* be felt. And it will kill your chances.

Neediness is a symptom of internal scarcity. It comes from believing you *lack* something—value, worth, options, or identity—and that a woman's interest in you is the missing piece. But this mindset not only sabotages your interactions, it also keeps you stuck in a cycle of approval-seeking, insecurity, and weak masculine energy.

To attract and keep high-value women, you must *eliminate neediness at the root*— not mask it, not fake confidence over it, but truly *transform it*. That starts with understanding what neediness looks like, where it comes from, and how to permanently dissolve it.

What Neediness Looks Like (Even When You Think You're Hiding It)

Neediness isn't just texting too much or coming on too strong. It's much deeper. It's the energy behind your actions—the subtle signals that say, "Please validate me."

Here's what neediness often looks like:

- **Over-pursuing**: Constantly initiating, texting, and trying to force a connection.

- **Overanalyzing**: Reading into every word, emoji, or response time.

- **People-pleasing**: Hiding your opinions to avoid conflict or gain approval.

- **Fear of loss**: Feeling anxious when you sense distance or disinterest.

- **Attachment to outcome**: Placing all your emotional weight on whether it "works out."

Even if you're saying the right things, your *vibe* tells the truth. Women—especially high-value women—are masters of reading subtle energy. If you don't value yourself, they'll sense it instantly, even if you're putting on a confident front.

Where Neediness Comes From

Neediness isn't a personality flaw—it's a byproduct of unmet needs. At its core, it comes from:

- **Lack of self-worth**: Believing you're not enough on your own.

- **Scarcity mindset**: Believing women, opportunities, or love are limited.

- **External validation addiction**: Needing others to tell you you're worthy.

- **Insecurity**: Measuring your value by how others respond to you.

To eliminate neediness, you need to stop looking outward for wholeness. You need to stop thinking a woman will "complete" you. She won't. No one will. That's your job.

How to Kill Neediness at the Root

Neediness doesn't disappear by trying harder to "act confident." It goes away when you become genuinely *fulfilled from within*. Here's how to start that transformation:

1. Build a Life You're Proud Of

When you're living with purpose—working on your goals, building your body, pursuing your mission—you naturally stop fixating on women. You're too focused on becoming the man you admire. The more fulfilled you are with your own life, the less desperate you'll be for someone else to make you feel worthy.

A man who has a mission never begs for attention—he commands it through presence.

2. Detach from the Outcome

Wanting a woman is natural. *Needing* her is not. The difference? *Attachment.* When you stop tying your self-worth to how an interaction turns out, you become free. You speak more boldly. You flirt more playfully. You hold eye contact without flinching. Why? Because you're unattached. You're not chasing a win—you're expressing yourself and letting the chips fall where they may.

The paradox? The less you care about the outcome, the more attractive you become.

3. Be Willing to Walk Away

The most powerful position a man can hold is the ability to walk away from anything that doesn't align with his values or standards. This isn't arrogance—it's self-respect. If you're constantly bending to keep someone interested, you're telling yourself *they have more value than you do.* Flip that dynamic.

Walking away isn't weakness. It's proof that you don't negotiate your self-worth.

4. Stop Over-Investing Early

Neediness often shows up as over-giving—compliments, attention, energy—without first seeing if she's earned it. Real value comes from *discernment.* Don't rush to prove yourself. Let her invest too. Let her show *you* who she is. Attraction is built on mutual value, not one-sided effort.

5. Connect to Abundance

One woman's interest (or lack of it) is not a measure of your worth. There are countless women in the world—many of whom would be thrilled to know the real you. When you truly believe there are *options*, you stop trying to force things with people who don't align. You stop chasing. You start *choosing*.

The New Frame: You Are the Source

To eliminate neediness, you must stop seeing others as the source of your happiness, and instead realize *you are the source*. You create your value. You determine your worth. And when you carry that truth into every interaction, women feel it.

You're no longer performing. You're no longer playing a role. You're being fully, unapologetically *you*—grounded, confident, and whole. That's magnetic. That's powerful. That's what high-value women are drawn to.

So let go of the need to impress. Let go of the desperation to be liked. Focus on being *aligned*, not approved. Because when you stop needing, you start leading—and that's when the game truly changes.

Developing Quiet Confidence Without Ego

Confidence doesn't need to shout. It doesn't need to brag, flex, or dominate a room to be felt. In fact, the most powerful form of confidence is often the quietest. It's a calm, steady presence that says *"I know who I am, I know what I bring, and I don't need to prove it."* This is the kind of confidence that high-value women are instinctively drawn to—the kind that's rooted in *certainty, not showmanship*.

On the other hand, ego tries to *look* confident but comes from insecurity. Ego is loud because it's compensating. It wants to be seen, admired, praised. But true masculine confidence—*quiet confidence*—requires no spotlight. It's self-validating. It doesn't seek approval. And it holds more power in a glance, a pause, or a simple truth than ego ever could with a thousand words.

51

Quiet Confidence vs. Ego: What's the Difference?

To build quiet confidence, you need to understand the difference between *authentic strength* and *ego-driven noise*. They look similar on the surface but are built on opposite foundations.

Quiet Confidence	Ego
Comes from self-assurance	Comes from insecurity
Speaks with clarity and intention	Talks excessively to impress
Comfortable with silence	Fills space to avoid discomfort
Accepts not knowing everything	Pretends to know it all
Grounded in purpose	Rooted in comparison and validation
Can lead or follow without attachment	Must dominate or be "right"

Quiet confidence isn't about being passive—it's about being *deliberate*. It's about owning your space without taking up everyone else's. It's the presence that causes people to lean in, not because you're demanding attention, but because your *energy* commands it.

Where Quiet Confidence Comes From

Quiet confidence is not a personality trait—it's a *muscle* you build through experience, self-awareness, and inner work. Here's what it's rooted in:

1. Self-Respect

You don't need to boast when you respect yourself. You don't need applause when you already know your worth. Self-respect is the internal compass that tells you, "I'm enough. I don't need to chase approval to feel seen."

2. Competence

You become more confident the more capable you become. Whether it's in conversation, your career, your physical health, or leadership, confidence grows through *reps*. You don't need to talk about how good you are when your results—and your presence—already prove it.

3. Emotional Control

Quiet confidence comes from *inner stillness*. It means you don't get rattled easily. You don't overreact to rejection, criticism, or unexpected turns. You remain composed—not because you're numb, but because you're centered.

4. Purpose

When you're aligned with a mission, a vision, or a higher goal, you don't get caught up in petty games. You move with direction. You stop caring what people think because you're too focused on what truly matters.

How to Cultivate Quiet Confidence Without Ego

Let's break it down into actionable steps:

☑ Listen More, Speak with Purpose

Don't speak to fill silence—speak to contribute. Ask thoughtful questions. Listen without needing to interrupt or outdo. When you do speak, do so with clarity, not performance. A man who doesn't rush to be heard is a man who knows his voice matters.

☑ Ground Yourself in Reality

You don't need to pretend. Drop the act. You don't need to be the funniest, smartest, or most impressive guy in the room. Be *real*. Be solid. A grounded man is 10x more attractive than one trying to be something he's not.

☑ Accept Imperfection

Confidence isn't the absence of flaws—it's being okay with them. The ego resists failure; quiet confidence learns from it. Own your mistakes. Laugh at yourself. Be honest when you don't know something. That's strength.

☑ Move With Intention

How you carry yourself matters. Your posture, your eye contact, your handshake, the way you sit or enter a room—it all communicates confidence. Do it with intention, not arrogance. Be fully present. People can feel it.

☑ Let Your Actions Speak

Don't tell people what you're going to do. Show them. Don't announce your value—*demonstrate it*. When you build a life of substance, confidence becomes a byproduct. You'll feel no need to convince anyone of your worth because your life is living proof.

The Energy That Attracts

High-value women aren't looking for a man who needs to be the loudest in the room. They're looking for a man who knows who he is—even in silence. Quiet confidence tells her you're not easily shaken, not easily swayed, and not easily impressed—because you've done the work. You're not here to perform. You're here to lead.

This is the masculine edge. The energy that says, *"I'm good with or without you, but I choose to bring you into my world."* That's not ego. That's power. That's quiet, confident strength—the kind that doesn't need to announce itself, because it's already known.

And that's the man you're becoming.

Practicing Assertiveness and Emotional Control

To become the kind of man who attracts and keeps high-value women, two traits must be etched into your identity: assertiveness and emotional control. These are not optional. These are non-negotiable traits of mature, grounded masculinity. Together, they form the bedrock of respect, attraction, and inner power.

Assertiveness is your ability to speak your truth—clearly, calmly, and confidently—without aggression, apology, or fear. Emotional control is your ability to stay composed and centered under pressure, to respond instead of react. Without these two, you'll be either a pushover or a loose cannon—both of which kill attraction and repel high-value women.

When a man lacks assertiveness, he becomes passive, submissive, and easy to dismiss. When he lacks emotional control, he becomes volatile, unstable, and difficult to trust. But when a man has both? He becomes *dangerous in the best way possible*. He becomes unshakable.

What Assertiveness *Is* (And What It's Not)

Assertiveness is not aggression. It's not domination. And it's definitely not manipulation.

Assertiveness is simply this: *standing firm in your truth while respecting the truth of others*. It means speaking up when something matters. It means saying "no" when a boundary is being crossed. It means owning your desires, your decisions, and your direction without asking for permission.

An assertive man doesn't wait to be invited. He doesn't shrink in the face of disagreement. And he doesn't tolerate disrespect, from others or from himself.

Examples of Assertiveness in Action:

- Telling a woman what you want instead of hinting or hoping she guesses.

- Calling out behavior that disrespects your values.

- Declining an invitation or a situation that doesn't align with your goals—without guilt.

- Stating your boundaries with calm conviction, not raised voices.

- Standing your ground when challenged but never needing to escalate.

High-value women are drawn to assertive men because they represent *leadership*. They know what they want. They communicate with clarity. They don't fold under pressure. And they create an emotional environment where she can trust his direction.

The Power of Emotional Control

While assertiveness gives you the voice to speak, emotional control gives you the strength to stay centered. It's what keeps you grounded when things go sideways. It's what allows you to lead under stress, stay composed during conflict, and remain unfazed when a woman tests your boundaries—which she *will*.

Make no mistake: emotional volatility is weakness. If you're easily triggered, quick to anger, or consumed by anxiety or jealousy, you give away your power. You become reactive instead of proactive. You start chasing control of external situations because you've lost control internally.

But emotional control doesn't mean suppression. It means mastery. It's not about being numb—it's about being *stable*.

Mastering emotional control looks like:

- Remaining calm when she challenges you or pulls away, instead of panicking or begging.

- Breathing and pausing before responding to triggers, rather than reacting impulsively.

- Accepting rejection or failure without losing your sense of self-worth.

- Letting go of what you can't control and doubling down on what you *can*—your focus, your habits, your standards.

How to Develop Assertiveness and Emotional Control

These aren't traits you're born with. They're skills. And like any skill, they're sharpened through intentional practice.

1. Get Comfortable with Discomfort

Assertiveness requires courage. You're going to feel tension when you speak up or stand firm. That's normal. Push through it. The more often you lean into discomfort, the more comfortable you become with owning your truth.

2. Use Direct Language

Stop sugarcoating. Speak plainly. Say what you mean without qualifiers. Replace "I was just wondering if maybe…" with "Here's what I want." Direct communication is respected. Vague, apologetic language is not.

3. Regulate Before You React

When emotions rise, slow everything down. Breathe. Check your body. Where is the tension? Where is the trigger coming from? This moment of awareness is the difference between emotional reactivity and emotional leadership.

4. Set and Enforce Boundaries

You teach people how to treat you by what you tolerate. Set boundaries that reflect your self-respect—and enforce them without drama. If someone crosses a line, address it once, clearly, and confidently.

5. Stand Alone if Necessary

Assertiveness and emotional control are tested when you're alone—when you're misunderstood, rejected, or walking away from something that doesn't serve you. Do it anyway. Stand tall. Walk with self-respect. A man who leads himself commands the world around him.

Final Word: Command Respect, Don't Demand It

The man who practices assertiveness and emotional control doesn't demand respect—he *commands* it. Not through fear. Not through force. But through *presence*. Through his ability to speak directly and stand strong, while staying emotionally grounded no matter what chaos the world—or a woman—throws at him.

This is the masculine edge that separates boys from men. And when you own it, you don't have to chase connection. You *create* it—on your terms.

So speak with conviction. Hold your frame. Lead from center. Because the man who leads *himself* is always the most attractive man in the room.

4

Mastering Your Masculine Frame

Understanding Polarity: Masculine vs. Feminine Energy

At the heart of all magnetic attraction lies a powerful, invisible force: **polarity**. It's the energetic tension between two opposing forces—*masculine and feminine energy*—that creates desire, chemistry, and connection. Just like a magnet, these two energies are drawn to each other not because they are the same, but because they are *different*. Understanding this dynamic is non-negotiable if you want to master your masculine frame and attract high-value women who are deeply feminine.

In every relationship, there is a dance of energy. And whether we're conscious of it or not, *polarity determines the intensity of that dance*. When polarity is strong, sparks fly. When polarity is weak or reversed, attraction dies—fast.

What Is Masculine Energy?

Masculine energy is about **direction, presence, and purpose**. It's steady, grounded, and focused. It's the part of you that leads, takes action, and holds structure. The masculine doesn't seek chaos—it brings order. It doesn't follow emotion—it anchors it.

Masculine energy says:

- *"I know where I'm going."*

- *"I've got this."*

- *"I don't need to be everything, but I will always show up as myself."*

At its core, the masculine is the **container**—the strong, solid force that holds space and moves forward with clarity and conviction.

Qualities of Masculine Energy:

- Leadership

- Logic and clarity

- Purpose and direction

- Discipline and focus

- Presence and stillness

- Grounded emotional control

When you're in your masculine frame, you're not performing—you're *embodying*. You don't chase. You don't shrink. You *hold*—your standards, your boundaries, your presence. And in doing so, you create the polarity that invites the feminine in.

What Is Feminine Energy?

Feminine energy is about **flow, expression, and emotion**. It's dynamic, spontaneous, and ever-changing. The feminine doesn't need a plan; it needs *presence*. It seeks to be felt, seen, and understood—not solved or controlled.

Feminine energy says:

- *"I want to be felt."*

- *"I move with emotion."*

- *"I respond to the strength of the container."*

At its core, the feminine is the **flow**—creative, emotional, and wild. Not in a chaotic sense, but in a deeply intuitive, feeling-driven way. It's not weak—it's powerful, and it responds only to a man strong enough to meet it without trying to tame it.

Qualities of Feminine Energy:

- Expression and feeling

- Creativity and intuition

- Nurturing and receiving

- Radiance and sensuality

- Spontaneity and emotional flow

When a woman is in her feminine, she doesn't want to *lead*—she wants to *feel led*. Not controlled, but *held* by a man who knows who he is and where he's going. That's the essence of polarity.

The Death of Attraction: When Polarity Collapses

Here's the truth most men don't understand: *sameness kills attraction*. When both people are in their masculine (constantly trying to lead, dominate, and control), the result is competition—not chemistry. When both are in their feminine (avoiding responsibility, indecisive, emotional), the result is instability—not safety or trust.

And when a man falls out of his masculine—when he becomes passive, emotionally erratic, or approval-seeking—he unconsciously forces the woman into her masculine to compensate. She starts leading. She starts protecting herself. She stops trusting you to hold the frame.

That's when attraction dies. Not because she stopped liking you—but because *you stopped embodying the masculine energy that invited her feminine to shine in the first place.*

How to Hold the Masculine Frame and Maintain Polarity

Mastering polarity starts with staying rooted in your masculine—*regardless* of what she's doing. You don't shift based on her emotions. You don't get pulled into her storm. You *remain the mountain*—still, strong, immovable.

Here's how you stay in your masculine and maintain polarity:

1. Lead with Purpose

Have direction in your life. Whether it's in conversation, your career, or a relationship, know where you're going. The feminine relaxes when she feels your purpose. Indecision kills polarity. Clarity *builds* it.

2. Stay Grounded in Emotionally Charged Moments

When she's emotional, she's not looking for you to fix her—she's testing to see if *you can handle her*. Don't panic. Don't argue. Stay calm. Listen, breathe, and *lead the energy*. That's strength.

3. Be the Structure to Her Flow

Let her be expressive, playful, emotional—that's the beauty of the feminine. Your job is not to suppress that—it's to *hold it*. Create a safe, steady frame for her to fully express herself without judgment or fear.

4. Don't Chase—Attract

Masculine energy doesn't need to chase approval or affection. It attracts through *presence*. Focus on being the man you admire. Build your life, your body, your mind. The more you embody your masculine core, the more you magnetize feminine energy to you.

Final Word: Polarity Is Your Edge

Polarity is the invisible engine of sexual energy and emotional connection. It's not about dominance—it's about *dynamic balance*. When you fully step into your masculine and hold your frame with quiet power, high-value feminine women will feel it instantly. They'll soften. They'll open. They'll follow—not because you forced them to, but because your energy gave them the freedom to.

Understand this: *You don't attract feminine energy by imitating it—you attract it by mastering your masculine*. When you embody leadership, direction, and grounded presence, polarity becomes effortless.

And once you understand how to create and maintain that polarity, you'll stop trying to convince women of your value… because they'll *feel it* the moment you walk into the room.

Strength, Presence and Direction as Core Masculine Traits

At the foundation of true masculine power are three unshakable traits: **strength**, **presence**, and **direction**. These aren't optional qualities—they are the backbone of your masculine frame. Without them, you'll constantly feel off-center, lost, or dependent on others—especially women—to define your value. But when you embody these traits, you become grounded, magnetic, and deeply attractive to high-value women.

Let's be clear: we're not talking about outdated stereotypes or surface-level bravado. We're talking about *embodied masculinity*—the kind that doesn't need to shout, impress, or force. These traits are not about being dominant over others; they're about becoming dominant over *yourself.*

1. Strength: Power With Purpose

Strength is more than physical. Yes, your body should be strong—your health, your discipline, your ability to endure pain and push through resistance all matter. But deeper than that is *inner strength*: the ability to stand firm in your values, your identity, and your truth when the world (or a woman) tries to test you.

A man with real strength is calm under pressure. He doesn't crumble when things get hard. He doesn't fold in the face of rejection or resistance. He's *resilient.* He's *reliable.* And because of that, he earns respect—without demanding it.

Ways to embody strength:

- Train your body. A strong man is a confident man. Lifting heavy, training consistently, and moving with power affect how you think and how others perceive you.

- Hold your boundaries. Don't let people cross your lines—especially in relationships. Enforce them calmly, not emotionally.

- Face discomfort. Whether it's emotional pain, financial pressure, or life challenges—lean into it. That's where real strength is forged.

2. Presence: The Power of Now

Presence is your ability to be fully *here*. Not distracted. Not anxious. Not trying to get somewhere else. Just *here*. This is a trait that's incredibly rare—and insanely attractive.

Most men are checked out. Stuck in their heads. Overthinking. Chasing results. But a man who is *present* doesn't need to try hard to impress—he *is* impressive, simply because his attention is powerful. When you bring your full awareness to the moment, people feel it. Women *feel* it. And they're drawn to it like gravity.

Presence makes you a leader. It makes you trustworthy. It makes you grounded in situations where others would lose their composure.

Ways to cultivate presence:

- Put your phone away when you're with people—especially women. Eye contact is presence. Active listening is presence. Your undivided attention is rare and valuable.

- Breathe. The breath is your anchor. When you feel reactive or distracted, come back to the breath. Inhale. Hold. Exhale. Reset.

- Meditate. Even 5 minutes a day of silence can sharpen your ability to stay grounded and aware in any situation.

3. Direction: Lead or Be Led

Direction is your compass. It's your vision. It's knowing who you are, where you're going, and what you're building—*with or without anyone else*. A man without direction is a man adrift, waiting for others (usually women) to give his life meaning. That's the fastest way to repel feminine energy and fall out of your masculine frame.

High-value women are not looking to become your purpose. They're looking to align with a man who *already has one*. Direction isn't about control—it's about *clarity*. When you move with purpose, others feel safe following you. Not because you're barking orders—but because you *know where you're going*.

Ways to develop direction:

- Get clear on your mission. What are you building in this life? It doesn't have to be grand yet—but it must be *real* to you.

- Make decisions quickly and confidently. Indecision is weakness. Even if you're wrong, course correction is better than standing still.

- Lead in your relationships. Plan the date. Set the tone. Guide the conversation. The masculine leads—not out of ego, but out of intent.

Final Word: The Masculine Edge

Strength. Presence. Direction. These aren't traits you switch on when you're trying to impress a woman. They're not techniques or pickup strategies. They are the *core of who you are becoming* as a masculine man.

When you live with strength, you are respected. When you lead with presence, you are felt. When you walk with direction, you are trusted. And when you combine all three, you don't just attract high-value women—you *naturally lead them* into your world.

This is your edge. This is your advantage. And it's something no one can give you, and no one can take away—because it's built from within.

How to Lead in Conversation, Dating and Life

Leadership isn't just about giving orders, being the loudest in the room, or forcing outcomes. True masculine leadership is subtle but powerful—it's about *guiding energy*, setting the tone, and creating direction in every interaction. Whether you're in a conversation, on a date, or designing your future, high-value women are instinctively drawn to men who *lead with clarity, confidence, and calm decisiveness.*

If you don't lead, she will—and while a feminine woman might temporarily step into that role, long-term, she'll lose trust in your frame. Leadership is your responsibility as a masculine man, and when done right, it invites the feminine to relax, respond, and lean into her natural essence.

Let's break down how to lead in the three critical areas: **conversation**, **dating**, and **life**.

1. How to Lead in Conversation

Every interaction is an opportunity to set the tone. Leading in conversation doesn't mean dominating the dialogue—it means creating *flow and depth.* You're the one who guides the direction, keeps things engaging, and isn't afraid to challenge, tease, or dig deeper when needed.

Key ways to lead in conversation:

- **Be intentional**: Don't ask surface-level questions just to fill silence. Go beyond small talk. Ask questions that matter—things that reveal values, stories, or insights.

- **Set the emotional tone**: If you're playful, grounded, and calm, she'll reflect that energy. If you're nervous or try-hard, she'll mirror that too. Set the vibe with your *state*, not your words.

- **Challenge, don't chase**: Don't be afraid to disagree or push back lightly. Confident teasing, playful resistance, and honest opinions show strength. You're not here to win her approval—you're here to *see if she fits your world.*

- **Control the frame**: If she throws a test, flirts with sarcasm, or pokes at you, don't get defensive. Smile, hold eye contact, and own the moment. Leading the frame means you stay centered, no matter what energy she brings.

2. How to Lead in Dating

Dating is where your leadership as a man becomes most obvious. A woman instantly senses whether you're a man who creates experiences—or one who waits to be led. Leadership in dating isn't about control—it's about *confidence and clarity*. You invite her into a world she wants to enter.

Key ways to lead in dating:

- **Plan with purpose**: Don't ask, *"What do you want to do?"* Instead, say, *"Let's grab a drink at this rooftop bar I know. 8 PM. I'll send you the address."* This shows decisiveness. She can always offer input, but you're the one initiating.

- **Move things forward**: You guide the pace. Whether it's escalating touch, building intimacy, or setting the next date, you take the lead. You're not rushing—but you're also not stalling, waiting for signs of permission.

- **Make decisions with conviction**: From where to sit to what to order, own your choices. Even if she doesn't agree with all of them, she'll respect that you *have a clear point of view*.

- **Create emotional safety**: Leadership means she can be vulnerable, playful, or feminine around you—because she trusts your groundedness. That safety is created through consistency, calm, and clear intent.

3. How to Lead in Life

The man who leads in life doesn't just chase women—he creates a life *so compelling*, women want to be part of it. This is about becoming a man of **vision, standards, and movement**. You lead yourself first. Always.

Key ways to lead in life:

- **Have a mission bigger than dating**: Your purpose is your anchor. Whether it's building a business, mastering a craft, or pursuing a long-term vision—this is what centers you. When you have direction, women feel it. You're not floating—you're *moving*.

- **Be decisive and proactive**: Don't wait for permission. Don't overthink. Make the call. Take the risk. Learn from the outcome. Leadership in life means you move forward while others hesitate.

- **Hold yourself to a higher standard**: You're not led by comfort or convenience—you're led by *discipline and alignment*. Your habits, choices, and circle of influence reflect your identity.

- **Lead by example**: You don't need to convince people of your value— you show them. The way you carry yourself, handle setbacks, and follow through on your word is what builds influence and respect.

Final Word: Leadership Is an Invitation

Leading isn't about forcing—it's about *inviting*. You lead the moment, the connection, and the future with calm certainty. You don't need applause. You don't seek approval. You're not trying to control outcomes—you're *owning your direction* and offering others the chance to come with you.

High-value women aren't looking for someone to tell them what to do. They're looking for a man they can *trust to lead*—because they know that behind his leadership is strength, vision, and integrity.

So lead the conversation. Lead the date. Lead your life. Not because you have to—but because a man who leads from truth doesn't follow anything less.

Building Boundaries and Non-Negotiables

If you don't set boundaries in life and relationships, someone else will—and it almost always leads to frustration, disrespect, and misalignment. As a man stepping into your masculine frame, you must understand this: **boundaries are not walls; they are standards.** They're how you protect your energy, time, values, and identity. And your *non-negotiables*? They're the lines you never cross— your internal code of conduct that keeps you grounded, focused, and self-respecting.

High-value women are drawn to men who know what they stand for—and *what they won't stand for*. If you're easily swayed, constantly people-pleasing, or too afraid to say "no" out of fear of losing connection, you're not in your masculine. You're in survival mode, seeking approval instead of living in alignment.

What Are Boundaries?

Boundaries are clear lines that define what you accept—and what you don't. They exist to protect your peace, reinforce your values, and maintain your sense of self. You don't need to yell them. You don't need to justify them. You simply *enforce them consistently*—with calm conviction.

In dating, weak boundaries look like:

- Tolerating disrespect or passive-aggressive behavior.

- Ignoring red flags because you're afraid of being alone.

- Over-giving to "prove" your worth.

- Letting attraction override your standards.

Strong boundaries, on the other hand, look like:

- Ending a date early if a woman is disrespectful.

- Saying no to sex, texting, or plans when it doesn't align with your energy or intentions.

- Walking away from a connection that compromises your values—no matter how attractive she is.

Boundaries are how you **teach others how to treat you**. And every time you enforce one, you reinforce your self-worth.

Non-Negotiables: Your Code of Integrity

Your *non-negotiables* are the core principles you will not compromise—regardless of emotions, pressure, or temptation. These aren't about ego; they're about **identity**. Who you are. What you will and won't allow into your world.

Some examples of masculine non-negotiables:

- I don't tolerate disrespect—from anyone.

- I don't chase women. I attract and lead.

- I don't explain my standards. I live by them.

- I don't stay in environments that kill my ambition or drain my peace.

- I don't betray my purpose for comfort, sex, or approval.

When you live by your non-negotiables, you don't need to broadcast them. People feel it. Women feel it. And the ones who are meant for you will respect you more for standing your ground—because your frame communicates strength, discipline, and self-respect.

How to Build and Enforce Boundaries

1. Define Your Standards

If you don't know your line, how can you defend it? Write down the top 5 values you refuse to compromise in relationships—things like honesty, emotional maturity, ambition, or mutual respect.

2. Practice Saying "No" Without Guilt

A strong man doesn't fear rejection or confrontation. If something violates your standards, decline it—calmly and directly. No justification needed.

3. Enforce With Action, Not Emotion

When a boundary is crossed, don't argue or debate. Take action. Leave. Disconnect. Reset. Your behavior sends a stronger message than words ever could.

4. Don't Apologize for Your Lines

You're not here to be liked by everyone—you're here to be respected by the right ones. Stop apologizing for expecting more. Your boundaries *filter out what doesn't belong.*

5. Revisit and Refine Your Non-Negotiables

As you grow, so will your standards. Keep evolving them based on your goals, experiences, and inner clarity.

Final Word: Boundaries Are Freedom

Most men think boundaries push people away. But the truth is: *boundaries pull the right people closer.* A high-value woman doesn't want a man she can walk all over. She wants a man who holds the line—because that line represents his strength, self-respect, and leadership.

When you know your non-negotiables and enforce your boundaries with calm, quiet conviction, you move from *needing connection* to *choosing alignment.* And that's when you become unstoppable—not just in dating, but in every area of your life.

Because the man who won't betray his standards for anyone... is the man everyone secretly respects.

Masculine Energy in a Hyper-Feminized World

We're living in a time where traditional masculinity is not just misunderstood—it's often discouraged, diluted, or outright demonized. In today's hyper-feminized world, emotional reactivity is rewarded over stoic clarity, validation-seeking has replaced vision, and men are being conditioned to abandon their edge in order to fit into a more "acceptable" version of themselves.

The result? A generation of men who are disconnected from their masculine core. Passive. Directionless. Starved for approval. And wondering why they feel unfulfilled and unattractive to the very women they want most.

Let's make one thing clear: masculine energy is not toxic—it's essential. Without it, society collapses. Without it, relationships lose their polarity. Without it, a man loses his purpose and power. The world may push you to suppress your masculinity, but if you want to lead, build, attract, and conquer, you must *reclaim it.*

What Is a Hyper-Feminized World?

A hyper-feminized world is one where emotional sensitivity is prioritized over reason, where comfort is valued more than challenge, and where assertiveness is confused with aggression. It's a culture that tells men to be "nice," "harmless," and "inoffensive"—stripping away the very traits that create strong, capable leaders.

Masculine energy in this context is often labeled "problematic," while submissiveness is praised as virtue. Men are taught to seek approval rather than earn respect, to avoid tension rather than confront it, and to defer rather than decide.

But here's the truth:

- The world doesn't need more nice guys. It needs more grounded *men*.

- Women aren't attracted to passive approval-seekers. They're drawn to men who own their masculine edge.

- The feminine doesn't feel safe with weakness. It flourishes in the presence of *strength, structure, and leadership*.

Reclaiming Your Masculine Energy

Masculine energy isn't about being emotionless or controlling—it's about being centered, purposeful, and unshakably grounded. In a world pushing softness, reclaiming your edge is an act of rebellion—and of leadership.

Here's how you reclaim and embody your masculine energy:

1. Get Ruthlessly Clear on Your Mission

Masculinity thrives on direction. Without purpose, you drift. You get distracted, emotional, reactive. Find your "why," then structure your life around it. Your mission isn't optional—it's your spine.

2. Disengage from the Validation Trap

Stop seeking approval. From women. From social media. From society. Masculine energy is *self-validating*. When you live in alignment with your truth, the right people will follow. The wrong ones will fall away.

3. Train Your Mind and Body to Be Strong

Strength isn't just about the gym—it's about becoming unbreakable under pressure. Train like your future depends on it. Because it does. A strong body leads to a sharp mind. A sharp mind leads to effective action.

4. Learn to Hold Emotional Space Without Becoming It

Feminine energy expresses and flows. Masculine energy *holds and contains*. You can feel emotions without being consumed by them. You don't suppress—*you manage*. That's true power.

5. Lead Without Apology

Don't shrink to make others comfortable. Don't play small to fit into a weak culture. Lead your life. Lead your relationships. Lead your environment. Masculine energy *guides, protects, and decides*.

The Cost of Suppressing Your Masculinity

When you dim your masculine light to please the world, you:

- Lose the respect of others—and yourself.

- Attract drama instead of devotion.

- Create confusion in romantic polarity.

- Feel lost, anxious, and resentful.

- Watch others lead lives you were meant to claim.

But when you turn your masculine energy *back on*—when you embrace strength, presence, and leadership—you not only transform your own life, you become the rarest man in the room. The kind of man who doesn't chase women, approval, or validation. He *draws them in*—because he radiates clarity in a world of chaos.

Final Word: Be the Antidote

This hyper-feminized world doesn't need more emotional reactivity. It needs *emotional leadership*. It doesn't need more soft, indecisive men trying not to offend—it needs strong, grounded, mission-driven men who lead with integrity and presence.

Be that man. Don't suppress your masculinity—*sharpen it*. In a world trying to blur the lines, you draw them. Boldly. Fearlessly. Unapologetically. Not to dominate—but to *stand for something real*. Because when you master your masculine energy, you become the antidote to a weak culture—and the kind of man high-value women recognize the moment you walk into the room.

5

Physical Excellence – Look the Part, Feel the Part

Why Looks Matter (More Than You Think)

L et's cut through the comforting lies and get brutally honest—**your looks matter**. More than you've been told. More than you might want to admit. In a world obsessed with internal value, personality, and "what's on the inside," one truth still remains unshakable: **your physical presence is the first thing the world—and women—see**. Before you open your mouth. Before you share your vision. Before you prove your worth.

That doesn't mean you have to be a fitness model, nor does it mean chasing superficial perfection. What it does mean is that your appearance is either a *weapon* working for you… or a *barrier* holding you back. And in the world of high-value dating and high-performance living, how you look is *either opening doors or closing them*. There is no neutral.

The Truth: Women Are Visual Too

Contrary to what you may have heard, women are not blind to looks. They might not focus solely on facial symmetry like men often do, but make no mistake—they're scanning everything:

- **Your physique** (Does he have discipline?)

- **Your posture** (Is he confident?)

- **Your grooming** (Does he respect himself?)

- **Your style** (Does he understand how to present himself?)

- **Your energy** (Does he look alive or drained?)

They can size you up in seconds. Not because they're shallow, but because they're wired to assess safety, status, and strength instantly. Your appearance sends signals—about your health, your habits, your self-worth, and your ability to *lead yourself.*

A well-built, well-dressed man who walks with intention doesn't need to say he's high-value. He *looks* high-value. He *moves* like it. He *embodies* it. And because of that, people—especially women—respond differently. They *respect* you without you needing to convince them.

Your Body Reflects Your Standards

A strong, lean, well-kept body says something loud and clear:

- "I show up for myself."

- "I respect the temple I live in."

- "I don't let comfort dictate my life."

- "I'm not afraid of pain, pressure, or progress."

Your physical condition is often a mirror of your **discipline**, and high-value women know it. The gym isn't just where you build muscle—it's where you *prove to yourself* that you can do hard things, consistently. And that mindset bleeds into every other area of life: dating, business, leadership, emotional control.

Style Is Strategy

You don't need to be a fashion expert to be well-dressed. You just need to **give a damn**. Your clothes tell people what you think of yourself before you say a word. Are you polished? Are you intentional? Or are you showing up like a man who's given up?

Good style doesn't mean wearing brands—it means wearing confidence. It means tailoring your image to fit your identity and goals. When your look is dialed in, you feel more powerful. That's not vanity—it's *strategy.*

Energy Is Visual

How you take care of yourself—physically, nutritionally, even hormonally—directly affects your *presence*. If you're tired, inflamed, bloated, or out of shape, it shows in your eyes, your skin, your posture, your vibe. A man who takes care of his body *radiates vitality*. He walks into the room with a full tank, not dragging his soul behind him.

People don't just see how you look—they *feel* how you live.

Final Word: The Outer Reflects the Inner

You can't claim to be a high-value man if you walk around like someone who's given up. You can't lead others if you can't lead your own body. Your physical appearance is not about vanity—it's about *alignment*. It's about integrity. It's about showing the world that you're the kind of man who *takes himself seriously*—and that's why the world should, too.

So train hard. Dress well. Move with power. Look like the man you want to be—because when you **look the part, you start to feel the part**. And when you feel the part, you show up with the kind of energy that makes everything in life—especially with women—bend in your favor.

Building a Body that Radiates Strength and Vitality

The body you build is not just a physical form; it's a reflection of your inner strength, discipline, and the way you show up in the world. A body that radiates strength and vitality sends a powerful message to everyone around you: *I take care of myself. I am disciplined. I am capable of overcoming challenges.* And more importantly, it becomes a magnet for success in all areas of life—dating, career, relationships, and personal fulfilment.

But building a body that exudes strength and vitality isn't about chasing aesthetics. It's about cultivating *longevity, power, and energy*—the kind of physical presence that commands respect and attracts high-value people into your orbit.

It's not about looking good for the sake of vanity, but about feeling good and knowing that every inch of your body is aligned with your highest standards.

The Foundation: Strength Over Aesthetics

Too many men make the mistake of prioritizing superficial aesthetics—six-pack abs, bigger biceps, a chiseled jawline—at the cost of overall health and strength. The problem? While these things can certainly boost your confidence and draw attention, they don't represent the full picture of *masculine power*.

Building strength should be the primary goal. Not just muscle definition, but real **functional strength**—the kind that shows up in your posture, your energy, and how you handle life's obstacles. Strength isn't just about lifting weights—it's about lifting yourself through the challenges that come your way, whether physical, mental, or emotional.

When you build strength, you also build resilience. You push past discomfort, you test your limits, and you gain a sense of mastery over your own body. This is the kind of strength that radiates, that inspires confidence and attracts high-value women and men alike. It's the kind of strength that doesn't need to flex to be seen—it *shows itself* in everything you do.

Vitality: Energy as Your Secret Weapon

Strength is the foundation, but **vitality is the spark**. It's the difference between a man who looks tired and sluggish, and a man who exudes energy, charisma, and magnetism.

Vitality comes from a few key elements:

- **Nutrition**: What you put into your body matters. A nutrient-dense, balanced diet full of whole foods fuels your energy, enhances your mood, and sharpens your focus. A body running on real food and proper hydration will have the stamina to conquer long days, intense workouts, and demanding situations. Avoid quick-fix diets that promise fast results but drain your energy in the long run. Opt for sustainable nutrition that supports both your body's performance and longevity.

- **Sleep**: Vitality is impossible to maintain without quality sleep. Sleep is the body's reset button, where recovery happens. When you're rested, you're sharp, present, and your body functions at its best. Prioritize sleep like you do any other workout—your body needs it to build strength, recover, and perform at its peak.

- **Recovery**: True vitality comes from knowing when to push hard and when to rest. Your body requires time to repair and rebuild itself after intense physical activity. Whether it's stretching, yoga, foam rolling, or simply taking a day off, recovery should be an essential part of your fitness routine.

- **Mind-Body Connection**: Vitality isn't just physical; it's mental. A strong mind creates a strong body. Meditation, mindfulness, and mental clarity exercises help you cultivate energy, focus, and stress resilience, which in turn boosts your physical performance.

Building a Body that Exudes Confidence

When you focus on strength and vitality, your body naturally reflects this in more than just muscle mass. It shows in your posture, your movements, and the way you carry yourself. Here's how to ensure that the strength and vitality you build truly *radiates*:

- **Posture**: A strong body is nothing without good posture. Stand tall, chest out, shoulders back. A man who owns his posture owns the room. This simple adjustment can change the way you're perceived by others. It signals confidence, authority, and presence.

- **Movement**: How you move is just as important as how you look. Walk with purpose. Whether it's in a meeting or on a date, every step should be purposeful. Be deliberate in how you navigate the world, as it's a direct reflection of how you feel about yourself.

- **Presence**: When you feel strong and vital, you radiate a magnetic presence. This is about more than just being physically noticeable—it's about owning your space. People are naturally drawn to men who exude a calm, centered energy, and this is a direct result of a body that's built for power and endurance.

Training for Longevity and Strength

The key to building a body that radiates strength and vitality is **training for longevity**. That means finding a fitness routine that isn't about short-term gains, but about creating a body that will continue to serve you for years to come.

- **Compound Movements**: Focus on exercises that engage multiple muscle groups, such as squats, deadlifts, bench presses, pull-ups, and rows. These compound movements build functional strength, increase muscle mass, and improve overall coordination.

- **Cardio**: Incorporate cardiovascular training into your routine to improve heart health, stamina, and endurance. Whether it's running, cycling, swimming, or HIIT, cardiovascular fitness keeps your energy levels high and supports your overall vitality.

- **Flexibility and Mobility**: Strength without flexibility is rigidity. Incorporate stretching, yoga, or mobility drills to keep your joints healthy, reduce injury risk, and ensure you have the full range of motion for every movement.

- **Consistency**: Results come from consistent, intelligent training. Be patient. Building strength and vitality is a long-term project, but the rewards are worth it.

Final Word: A Body that Commands Respect

A body that radiates strength and vitality is more than just a superficial asset—it's a direct reflection of your character, your discipline, and your willingness to show up for yourself. It signals to the world that you don't just survive—you *thrive*.

When you dedicate yourself to building strength and nurturing vitality, you not only improve your physical presence—you elevate your entire life. You feel more powerful. More confident. More capable of tackling the challenges that come your way. You become a man who others respect, and one who women instinctively want by their side.

This is the body that draws people in. This is the body that moves with purpose. This is the body of a man who has decided to live at his highest potential. **Build it. Cultivate it. Own it.**

Style, Grooming and Personal Brand 101

In a world where first impressions are often the only impression, how you present yourself matters more than ever. Your **style, grooming, and personal brand** are not just superficial details—they are the signals you send to the world about your value, your identity, and how seriously you take yourself. They are your visual language, the first clues to who you are before you even speak a word.

Mastering these elements isn't about trying to impress people with the latest trends or spending a fortune on designer labels. It's about cultivating an image that aligns with your masculinity, your purpose, and your self-respect. It's about showing up as a man who is dialed in, who understands the importance of presentation, and who leverages this awareness to elevate his life.

Style: Dressing with Purpose

Your clothes do more than cover your body—they communicate your identity. **Style is your silent statement**. It's how you express who you are without saying a word. Whether you're heading to a business meeting, a date, or simply running errands, your clothing should reflect your **standards**, **values**, and **confidence**.

Key Principles for Mastering Style:

1. **Fit Over Fashion**: The most expensive clothes can look cheap if they don't fit properly. Focus on well-tailored clothes that flatter your body shape. A good fit will elevate your entire appearance and make you look more put-together and sharp.

2. **Quality Over Quantity**: Invest in a few high-quality, versatile pieces that will last rather than overloading your wardrobe with trends. Classic items like a crisp white shirt, dark jeans, tailored suits, and a well-fitted blazer never go out of style. They're timeless.

3. **Define Your Aesthetic**: Your style should be an extension of who you are, not a forced attempt to fit into a particular category. Whether you prefer a minimalist look, a rugged vibe, or a polished, professional aesthetic, **authenticity** is key. Choose clothing that makes you feel comfortable and confident.

4. **Details Matter**: The small touches can make all the difference. **Well-chosen accessories**, such as a sleek watch, quality shoes, or a leather belt, can elevate your look. These elements communicate attention to detail and an understanding of style.

5. **Dress for the Occasion**: Knowing how to dress for different situations shows that you are aware of social dynamics. A casual look might be appropriate for a laid-back date, but a more polished appearance will be necessary for business or a formal event. Adapt to your environment without sacrificing your identity.

Grooming: Mastering the Basics

Your grooming habits are a direct reflection of your self-respect and discipline. How you take care of your skin, hair, and overall cleanliness shows the world how much you value yourself and how seriously you take your appearance.

Key Grooming Tips:

1. **Hair**: A clean, well-maintained haircut is non-negotiable. Find a hairstyle that suits your face shape and lifestyle. Whether you opt for a fresh fade, a clean buzz, or a more styled look, make sure it's well-kept and suits your aesthetic. Regular trims are a must to keep it sharp.

2. **Skin**: Healthy skin is a sign of vitality. Invest in a basic skincare routine—cleanser, moisturizer, and sunscreen. Clear, glowing skin doesn't just improve your physical appearance; it also shows that you

take care of yourself. And remember, **less is often more**. A simple, minimal skincare routine is all you need to look your best.

3. **Facial Hair**: Whether you prefer a clean-shaven face or sport facial hair, ensure it's neat. If you have a beard, keep it trimmed and shaped to suit your face. A well-groomed beard can exude strength and masculinity, but a messy one sends a different message. Pay attention to details, like trimming stray hairs and maintaining clean edges.

4. **Nails and Hands**: Your hands and nails are often overlooked, but they play a crucial role in your grooming. Keep your nails trimmed and clean. If you're into fitness or have a physically demanding lifestyle, make sure to moisturize your hands and cuticles regularly. It's a small touch that makes a big impact.

5. **Fragrance**: A good fragrance is a subtle yet powerful tool in your grooming arsenal. Choose a scent that complements your personality and doesn't overpower. A signature scent will leave a lasting impression, but it should be subtle, not overwhelming.

Personal Brand: Your Identity in the World

Your **personal brand** is the sum of how you present yourself to the world—it's what people think of when they think of you, both in person and online. It's how you craft your image, communicate your values, and project your confidence, all of which combine to create your *reputation*.

Building a Personal Brand:

1. **Clarity of Purpose**: Know who you are and what you stand for. Your personal brand is built on your values, your mission, and how you show up in the world. A man with a clear purpose is magnetic. Women, business partners, and people in your circle will be drawn to you because of your vision and your ability to articulate it.

2. **Consistency**: Your style, grooming, and behavior need to align with the brand you're creating. If you're polished and confident in person but inconsistent online, people will question your authenticity. Stay consistent in how you present yourself, both in the physical world and

on social media. Your online persona should reflect the same energy and values as your real-life interactions.

3. **Confidence in Your Identity**: Own who you are. A man who is comfortable in his own skin, who isn't trying to be someone he's not, naturally attracts respect. The most important part of your personal brand is your confidence—believing in yourself enough to stand firm in your decisions, style, and values.

4. **Social Proof**: Surround yourself with other high-value people who align with your brand. A strong network enhances your personal brand. The relationships you nurture and the people you choose to associate with will elevate your status and amplify the impact of your brand.

5. **Crafting Your Narrative**: Your personal brand is also about the story you tell. This goes beyond what you wear or how you look—it's how you present yourself to others through your words, your actions, and your decisions. Craft your narrative thoughtfully, and make sure it reflects the high standards you set for yourself.

Final Word: Own Your Image

Style, grooming, and personal brand are not optional for the man who seeks excellence—they are the bedrock of how you are perceived and how you feel about yourself. They create alignment between your inner confidence and outer presentation. And when you are aligned, you radiate power.

Own your image. Take pride in your style. Be meticulous in your grooming. And most importantly, build a personal brand that speaks to your highest potential. When you do, you'll not only attract what you want—you'll become the man others naturally look up to.

Health, Testosterone and Vital Masculine Energy

When you think of masculinity, what comes to mind? Strength, confidence, leadership, the ability to protect and provide—these traits are deeply rooted in our biology. They are a direct reflection of our **masculine energy**, which is influenced by a multitude of factors. One of the most critical components of this energy is **testosterone**—the hormone that drives much of what we associate with masculinity. But testosterone alone doesn't make you a man; it's how you *manage* and *optimize* your health and vitality that determines how powerfully you express your masculine energy in the world.

Testosterone is more than just a "male hormone." It's the biological foundation for everything from muscle growth to mood, from motivation to libido. But in today's world, where stress, sedentary lifestyles, and poor nutrition are rampant, too many men are seeing a decline in their testosterone levels, leading to a drop in energy, mood, and overall vitality.

The good news? **You can take control.** Health, testosterone, and masculine energy are interwoven—and by prioritizing certain habits and lifestyle choices, you can optimize your health, elevate your testosterone, and unlock the vitality that powers your masculinity.

Testosterone: The Lifeblood of Masculine Energy

Testosterone is the hormone that gives men their edge. It influences not just physical traits—like muscle mass, body composition, and facial hair—but also mental and emotional aspects of masculinity, like aggression, motivation, and resilience.

It's also what fuels your **vitality**. Low testosterone levels are linked to decreased energy, increased body fat, reduced muscle mass, and a general sense of fatigue or apathy. It can lead to feeling like you're running on empty, even when you've had a full night's sleep. Testosterone, when optimized, **fuels the fire** of your masculinity, giving you the strength to take on challenges, the energy to pursue your goals, and the clarity to make decisions with confidence.

The Decline of Testosterone in Modern Life

The unfortunate reality is that **testosterone levels are declining** in men worldwide. Studies have shown that testosterone levels in men have decreased by nearly 1% per year since the 1980s, and this decline is linked to lifestyle factors such as:

- **Sedentary behavior**: Spending too much time sitting and not enough time moving or lifting weights.

- **Poor diet**: Diets high in processed foods, sugars, and unhealthy fats can disrupt hormone production.

- **Chronic stress**: High stress increases cortisol, which directly suppresses testosterone.

- **Sleep deprivation**: Poor or insufficient sleep prevents testosterone levels from reaching their peak during recovery.

This decline in testosterone doesn't just affect your physical health—it also impacts your energy, your confidence, and your ability to thrive in the world. You might feel sluggish, disconnected, or less motivated to go after your goals. This is where taking charge of your **health** becomes crucial.

Optimizing Testosterone and Vitality

You don't need to be a biohacker or spend a fortune on supplements to optimize your testosterone and regain your masculine energy. The **foundation** of healthy testosterone levels is rooted in **lifestyle choices**. Here's how you can support healthy testosterone production and maintain that vital masculine energy:

1. **Exercise and Strength Training**: Resistance training, such as weightlifting, is one of the most effective ways to boost testosterone. Compound movements (like squats, deadlifts, and bench presses) engage multiple muscle groups and trigger the release of growth hormone and testosterone. Aim for 3-5 strength training sessions per week.

2. **High-Intensity Interval Training (HIIT)**: In addition to weight training, incorporating short bursts of intense cardio (HIIT) can also increase testosterone levels. HIIT has been shown to be particularly effective in raising testosterone levels, improving cardiovascular health, and enhancing fat loss.

3. **Nutrition**: What you eat directly impacts your hormones. Focus on a balanced, nutrient-dense diet with an emphasis on:

   o **Healthy fats**: Avocados, olive oil, nuts, seeds, and fatty fish are crucial for testosterone production.

   o **Lean proteins**: Grass-fed beef, free-range chicken, eggs, and wild-caught fish provide the amino acids needed for muscle repair and testosterone production.

   o **Micronutrients**: Zinc and vitamin D are particularly important for healthy testosterone levels. Include zinc-rich foods like oysters, pumpkin seeds, and spinach, and ensure you're getting enough vitamin D through sunlight or supplements.

4. **Sleep Like a King**: Testosterone is produced during deep sleep, particularly during the REM stage. Prioritize 7-9 hours of quality sleep each night to ensure your body can regenerate and produce optimal levels of testosterone. Avoid excessive blue light before bed and create a sleep-friendly environment—cool, dark, and quiet.

5. **Reduce Stress**: Chronic stress increases cortisol, a hormone that directly blocks testosterone production. High cortisol levels can make you feel drained, anxious, and demotivated. Incorporate stress-reducing habits into your life such as mindfulness, meditation, deep breathing, or simply taking time to relax. Learning to manage stress effectively is crucial for keeping testosterone levels in check.

6. **Limit Alcohol and Toxins**: Excessive alcohol consumption and exposure to environmental toxins (like BPA in plastics) can lower testosterone levels. Limit your alcohol intake to occasional use, and be mindful of products you use that may contain endocrine-disrupting chemicals. Your body is a temple—protect it.

Mental and Emotional Health: The Testosterone Connection

Testosterone isn't just about physical power; it plays a key role in **emotional resilience** and **mental clarity**. Men with healthy testosterone levels tend to experience better mood regulation, greater confidence, and increased motivation. However, when testosterone dips, it's common to experience feelings of irritability, low libido, lack of focus, and even depression.

To ensure you're mentally sharp and emotionally stable, take care of your **mindset**:

- Practice **gratitude** and focus on positive outcomes.

- **Challenge yourself** daily—whether through physical, mental, or emotional tests.

- Cultivate a growth mindset that encourages learning and progress.

- Surround yourself with a **strong support network** of like-minded men and high-value individuals.

The Benefits of Vital Masculine Energy

When you take control of your health, optimize your testosterone, and prioritize your vitality, you unlock a well of masculine energy that fuels all aspects of your life:

- **Confidence**: You carry yourself with strength and clarity.

- **Motivation**: You wake up every day with a clear sense of purpose and drive.

- **Charisma**: Your presence demands attention because you're not just physically strong, but emotionally and mentally sharp.

- **Attractiveness**: Women and men alike are drawn to the energy you project—the vitality and self-assurance that radiates from you.

Final Word: Own Your Masculine Energy

Health, testosterone, and vitality are the pillars of a life filled with energy, purpose, and high performance. Your **masculine energy** is your natural force—it's the strength that propels you toward your goals, the confidence that powers your presence, and the vitality that enables you to take action without hesitation.

By optimizing your testosterone through focused health habits and maintaining a lifestyle that promotes strength and vitality, you don't just look the part—you **feel** the part. And when you feel the part, you step into your true masculine power, becoming the man who not only commands respect but also lives with unstoppable energy, passion, and purpose.

Daily Rituals that Signal Self-Respect

Self-respect is the cornerstone of a high-value man. It's the quiet, unshakable foundation on which you build your life, and it begins with how you treat yourself on a daily basis. The way you show up for yourself in the little moments, the routines you establish, and the rituals you follow tell the world more about your character than any words ever could. A man who respects himself acts with integrity, discipline, and purpose every single day, even when no one is watching.

Your **daily rituals** are not just habits—they're the behaviors that define your identity. They set the tone for your day, reinforce your values, and cultivate a mindset of high regard for yourself. In short, your rituals are a powerful expression of how much you value your time, your energy, and your potential. If you want to live a life filled with respect, both from others and from yourself, it starts with these key rituals.

1. Start Your Day with Purpose: Morning Rituals that Empower

The way you start your day sets the tone for everything that follows. If you begin your morning in a rushed, chaotic, or unfocused way, it's hard to feel grounded or centered. But if you start with intention, clarity, and focus, your entire day will carry that energy.

How to build your morning ritual:

- **Wake up early**: Successful men respect their time and understand that early mornings are a secret weapon. Waking up before the world gets noisy allows you to take control of your day and sets the stage for productivity.

- **Hydrate**: Drinking water as soon as you wake up rehydrates your body after a night's sleep and gives you an energy boost. It's a simple act, but it's one that signals respect for your health and vitality.

- **Meditate or Journal**: Spend a few minutes in meditation or journaling to clear your mind, focus your thoughts, and align your intentions for the day. This ritual cultivates mental clarity and emotional discipline—two qualities that show you value your peace of mind.

- **Move your body**: Whether it's a full workout, a brisk walk, or stretching, getting your body moving early in the morning ensures you start the day with energy. This doesn't just build physical strength—it signals to yourself that you're ready to take on whatever comes your way.

- **Eat a nutritious breakfast**: A balanced, nutritious breakfast sets the tone for the rest of your day. You don't need to make it elaborate, but a meal that fuels your body with protein, healthy fats, and fiber reflects your commitment to your health.

2. Stay Organized and Prioritize: Rituals for Productivity

A man who respects himself doesn't just go through the motions—he lives with purpose. Daily rituals that enhance your productivity help you stay focused on your goals, make smarter decisions, and avoid wasting time or energy on trivial matters.

How to build your productivity ritual:

- **Plan your day the night before**: Before you go to bed, take a few minutes to review your schedule for the next day. Having a clear plan in place allows you to wake up with direction and intention. When you start your day knowing exactly what you need to accomplish, you're less likely to get sidetracked.

- **Focus on high-impact tasks**: The most successful men understand the importance of working on the tasks that move the needle. Instead of procrastinating or getting caught up in distractions, prioritize the actions that will have the greatest impact on your goals.

- **Use time blocks**: Break your day into focused blocks of time where you work on specific tasks, and allow yourself short breaks between them. This method not only increases efficiency but also signals respect for your own attention span and mental capacity.

- **Keep your space clean and organized**: A cluttered space can lead to a cluttered mind. By keeping your environment tidy and organized, you demonstrate self-respect and discipline. An organized workspace is conducive to focused work and creativity.

3. Physical Care: Rituals that Honor Your Body

A man who respects himself knows that his body is his vessel in this world. He honors it by maintaining it, nurturing it, and treating it with the care it deserves. **Physical self-respect** is more than just a matter of appearance—it's about feeling strong, energetic, and confident in your own skin.

How to build your physical care ritual:

- **Exercise regularly**: Consistent exercise is not just about looking good, it's about feeling good and taking care of your health. It's an act of self-respect because it shows you're willing to invest in your well-being and longevity.

- **Grooming and hygiene**: Personal grooming is an essential ritual that speaks volumes about how you see yourself. Regular haircuts, shaving or trimming facial hair, and maintaining personal hygiene are basic rituals that show you care about your appearance and self-presentation.

- **Nutrition**: Treating your body with respect means fueling it with the right food. Eat whole, nutrient-dense foods that give you the energy and vitality to perform at your best. Avoid foods that drain you or leave you sluggish. Every meal should be an opportunity to honor your body and what it's capable of.

- **Sleep and recovery**: Rest is just as important as work. Prioritize quality sleep to allow your body to recover and recharge. A man who respects himself recognizes that proper rest is necessary to maintain peak performance.

4. Emotional Mastery: Rituals for Inner Strength

True self-respect isn't just about the physical; it's about mastering your emotional state and mental clarity. Your emotions are powerful, but they should never dictate your actions. When you master your emotions, you maintain control over your responses and behavior, no matter the situation.

How to build your emotional mastery ritual:

- **Mindfulness and meditation**: Start or end your day with a brief meditation or mindfulness practice. This helps you stay grounded and centered throughout the day, preventing emotional highs and lows from derailing your focus or composure.

- **Self-reflection**: Take time daily to reflect on your actions, thoughts, and behaviors. Journaling can help you process emotions, release stress, and make improvements for the future. Self-reflection is a ritual that signals you are actively working on your personal growth.

- **Set healthy boundaries**: A man who respects himself knows when to say "no" and when to say "yes." Setting boundaries—whether in relationships, work, or social settings—protects your time, energy, and emotional well-being. Respecting your own limits is crucial for maintaining your integrity.

5. Evening Rituals: Wind Down with Intent

How you end your day is just as important as how you start it. Evening rituals provide a sense of closure, allowing you to reflect on your accomplishments and prepare for rest. A well-planned evening ritual signals to yourself that you respect your body's need for rest and recovery, and it sets the stage for a productive tomorrow.

How to build your evening ritual:

- **Review your day**: Take a moment to reflect on what you accomplished. Acknowledge your wins, no matter how small, and consider what you could improve. This practice reinforces self-respect by celebrating progress and learning from setbacks.

- **Unplug from screens**: Avoid electronics an hour before bed. The blue light from screens can disrupt your sleep cycle and hinder your ability to rest fully. Instead, wind down with a good book, a calming routine, or light stretching.

- **Prepare for the next day**: Organize your clothes, plan meals, or write out your top priorities for tomorrow. This shows self-respect by easing morning stress and giving you a head start on the next day.

Final Word: Rituals Are the Foundation of Respect

The rituals you choose to follow each day are a direct reflection of how you view yourself. **Self-respect is a daily practice**—it's not something you achieve and then forget about; it's something you nurture, honor, and reinforce with every action you take. Your daily rituals should elevate you, challenge you, and reflect the high standards you set for yourself.

When you incorporate these rituals into your life, you're not just signaling to others that you respect yourself—you're showing *yourself* that you are worthy of respect, care, and investment. Over time, these rituals become habits that form the foundation of a high-value life—a life filled with confidence, strength, and integrity.

6

Social Skills & Charisma – Learning to Connect Authentically

Breaking Social Anxiety and Rewiring Confidence

Social anxiety is one of the most common barriers men face when it comes to connecting with others, especially when it comes to meeting new people, dating, or stepping into unfamiliar social situations. It can feel like an invisible wall that holds you back from showing the world the best version of yourself. The good news? **Social anxiety is not permanent**. With the right approach and consistent effort, you can break free from its grip and **rewire your brain** to experience confidence in social settings.

At its core, social anxiety is a learned response to certain situations. Your brain associates social interactions with discomfort, self-doubt, and fear of judgment. Over time, this can become a default state, causing you to second-guess yourself or even avoid social situations altogether. But this pattern is **not who you are—** it's just a habit your mind has formed over time. The key is to recognize this pattern and then **actively work to rewire** your brain for confidence.

1. Understanding Social Anxiety: The Biology of Fear

Before you can break through social anxiety, it's important to understand **why** it happens. Social anxiety stems from the **fight-or-flight response**, a survival mechanism that has evolved to protect you from perceived threats. When you're in a social situation, especially one where you're unsure of how you'll be received, your brain can misinterpret this as a potential danger, triggering feelings of discomfort, nervousness, and self-doubt.

However, in most social situations, these feelings of anxiety are **not real threats**—they're exaggerated responses to what you perceive could happen. By consciously **re-framing** these thoughts, you can teach your brain that social interactions are safe and even enjoyable.

2. The First Step: Awareness and Acceptance

The path to overcoming social anxiety begins with **awareness** and **acceptance**. Acknowledge that you experience anxiety, but don't define yourself by it. It's easy to fall into the trap of thinking, "I'm just an anxious person," but that's simply not true. You are someone who experiences anxiety in social situations, but that's only one part of who you are.

Once you accept that social anxiety is just a feeling—and not your identity—you create space for transformation. **Self-compassion** is a vital tool here. Be kind to yourself when you feel anxious. Recognize that it's a normal human response and that overcoming it is a gradual process.

3. Rewiring Your Confidence: Small Wins Lead to Big Change

The key to breaking free from social anxiety is **consistency**. Every time you put yourself in a social situation, you are actively **rewiring** your brain. By taking small steps outside your comfort zone, you can create a series of "wins" that build your confidence over time.

Here's how to start:

- **Start small**: If you feel nervous about meeting new people, begin with low-stakes situations. It might be striking up a short conversation with a cashier, saying hello to a neighbor, or asking someone a simple question in a public place. These are low-pressure interactions that give you the chance to practice being social.

- **Practice non-verbal confidence**: Your body language speaks volumes, even before you say a word. Work on projecting confidence through posture—stand tall, make eye contact, and smile. Research shows that

"acting confident" can trigger a feeling of confidence in your body, even if you don't feel confident at first.

- **Focus on others, not yourself**: Social anxiety often stems from overthinking how others perceive you. A great way to shift the focus away from your anxiety is to focus on **connecting with the other person**. Instead of worrying about how you look or what you're going to say, shift your attention to understanding and engaging with them. Ask questions, listen actively, and be genuinely curious. This takes the pressure off you and puts you in a place of connection, not performance.

- **Exposure therapy**: Gradually expose yourself to more challenging social situations. Start with small groups, then work your way up to larger gatherings or more formal settings. The more you expose yourself to these situations, the more you'll desensitize your brain to the anxiety and increase your confidence. Each step forward builds a new layer of **self-assurance**.

4. Reframing Negative Thoughts: Cognitive Restructuring

One of the most powerful tools in rewiring confidence is learning to **reframe** your negative thoughts. Social anxiety often involves automatic, self-criticizing thoughts like, "They'll think I'm awkward," or, "I'm not interesting enough." These thoughts can create a vicious cycle of self-doubt and avoidance.

Reframing involves challenging those thoughts and replacing them with healthier, more balanced perspectives. Instead of assuming the worst, try asking yourself:

- What's the worst that can happen? Most likely, it's not as bad as your mind is making it out to be.

- What's a more realistic outcome? It's more likely that people will find you genuine and interesting, not judgmental.

- What can I learn from this situation? Even if you don't nail the conversation, every social interaction is an opportunity for growth.

By changing the narrative in your mind, you shift from a place of fear to one of **empowerment**. The more you practice this, the less control anxiety will have over you.

5. Build a Confidence Routine: Make It Part of Your Lifestyle

Confidence isn't just a feeling—it's a **lifestyle**. To truly break free from social anxiety and rewire your brain, you need to make confidence a daily habit. Here are some practical ways to integrate confidence-building into your routine:

- **Physical activity**: Regular exercise releases endorphins and promotes a sense of well-being, which naturally boosts your confidence. Whether it's lifting weights, running, or doing yoga, being physically active will make you feel more empowered in your body, which translates into more confidence in social situations.

- **Positive self-talk**: The words you say to yourself matter. Every morning, affirm that you are capable, worthy, and worthy of respect. Start each day with a positive mantra or affirmation that sets the tone for your interactions.

- **Visualization**: Before you enter any social situation, visualize yourself feeling confident and having successful interactions. Picture yourself engaging with others effortlessly, laughing, and feeling at ease. This exercise primes your brain for success and reduces feelings of anxiety.

- **Celebrate progress**: Don't wait until you feel "perfect" to celebrate. Every small success—whether it's making conversation with someone new, attending a social event, or simply showing up—is a win. The more you acknowledge these wins, the more you reinforce your belief in your ability to connect.

6. Embrace Vulnerability: Confidence is Built on Connection

Finally, remember that confidence is not about being perfect or fearless—it's about **embracing vulnerability**. In social situations, confidence comes from being comfortable with who you are, flaws and all. People are drawn to authenticity, and the more you allow yourself to be genuine, the more others will gravitate toward you.

Social anxiety often stems from a fear of rejection or judgment. But the truth is, everyone feels a little uncertain at times. When you embrace your imperfections and show up with honesty, you invite others to do the same. Vulnerability creates **true connection**, and that is the ultimate confidence booster.

Final Word: Confidence is a Skill, Not an Inherited Trait

Breaking free from social anxiety is a process, not an overnight transformation. It requires consistent effort, self-compassion, and a commitment to rewiring your brain. The good news is that confidence is a skill, not something you're born with. Every step you take to break through your anxiety, to face discomfort, and to show up authentically brings you closer to becoming the confident, charismatic man you're meant to be.

Embrace the journey. With each social interaction, you are shaping your self-image and reinforcing your ability to connect with others. The more you practice, the more confident you'll become.

The Power of Eye Contact, Voice Tone and Body Language

When it comes to **social skills** and **charisma**, the impact of non-verbal communication cannot be overstated. In fact, studies show that **up to 93% of communication** is non-verbal, relying on subtle cues like eye contact, body language, and the tone of your voice. These elements can be more powerful than the words you speak. Mastering these aspects of your communication will not only help you **connect authentically** with others but will also amplify your **charisma** and presence in any social situation.

1. Eye Contact: The Window to Confidence and Connection

Eye contact is one of the most immediate and powerful ways to communicate with others. It's a sign of **confidence, respect**, and **attention**, and it plays a critical role in building rapport and trust. When you meet someone's gaze, you're signaling that you are **fully present** and engaged, which is one of the most magnetic qualities you can project in a conversation.

However, there's a balance to strike. Too little eye contact can make you seem disconnected or anxious, while too much can come across as **intense** or even confrontational. The key is to find a natural, comfortable level of eye contact that conveys your interest without overwhelming the other person.

- **Establishing the right level of eye contact**: In casual conversation, try to hold eye contact for about **3–5 seconds** before looking away. This shows you're engaged but doesn't make the other person feel uncomfortable. When listening, it's especially important to maintain eye contact as it signals that you're actively paying attention. If you're the one speaking, making eye contact will give your words more weight and authority.

- **Breaking eye contact**: Don't worry about holding eye contact the entire time. It's natural to look away occasionally. In fact, people often find it more comfortable when you break eye contact briefly and return to it. It's the rhythm of engaging and disengaging that feels natural.

- **Eye contact in groups**: In a group conversation, try to establish **"contact points"** with various individuals, making sure each person feels included. This makes the interaction feel more personal and gives off the impression that you're confident and comfortable within the group.

2. Voice Tone: The Unspoken Power of Your Words

Your voice is an incredibly powerful tool in communicating confidence and authority. The tone, pace, and volume of your speech can significantly impact how your words are received. **Voice tone** communicates more than the content of what you say—it conveys **emotion**, **intent**, and **energy**. A well-controlled, warm, and authoritative tone creates an aura of **command**, whereas a shaky or monotone voice can undermine your message and make you seem unsure of yourself.

- **Tone**: A steady, strong voice exudes confidence. If your voice cracks or wavers, it can make you appear anxious or unprepared. Practice speaking with a lower, more grounded tone. This doesn't mean speaking in a monotone, but rather with **clarity** and **certainty**. A confident tone commands attention, encourages engagement, and projects authority.

- **Pacing and rhythm**: Speaking too quickly can make you sound nervous or rushed, while speaking too slowly can cause the listener to lose interest. The key is to find a natural rhythm that allows your words to resonate. Pausing for a moment after important points can help create impact, and it also gives your audience a moment to absorb what you're saying.

- **Volume**: A voice that is too soft may be perceived as lacking in confidence or authority, while speaking too loudly can come across as overbearing or aggressive. The right volume varies depending on the environment, but in general, a voice that's **clear** and **projected** without being overpowering will always serve you well.

3. Body Language: The Silent Indicator of Your Inner State

Your body language is perhaps the most telling indicator of how you feel inside. It communicates your **level of comfort, confidence**, and **authenticity** without you ever having to say a word. Whether you're in a conversation, a meeting, or a date, your posture, movements, and gestures can say volumes about you.

- **Posture**: Standing tall with your shoulders back and your head held high is a sign of confidence. **Slouching** or **hunching** over can make you appear insecure, closed off, or disinterested. Keep your posture open and **assertive**—this signals that you're engaged, capable, and present. A strong, upright posture also has the added benefit of making you feel more confident and energized.

- **Open vs. Closed Body Language**: **Open body language** is welcoming and conveys trustworthiness and approachability. This can include keeping your arms uncrossed, standing with your legs slightly apart, and facing the person you're speaking with. **Closed body language**, on the other hand—such as crossed arms, turning your body away from someone, or avoiding eye contact—can indicate defensiveness, disinterest, or discomfort. If you want to attract and maintain others' attention, always aim for openness in your body language.

- **Gestures**: Using hand gestures while speaking can add emphasis to your words and make you appear more dynamic. However, excessive gestures or erratic movements can be distracting. Keep your hand gestures purposeful, natural, and in sync with the rhythm of your speech. **Subtle movements**, like leaning forward slightly to show interest, can create a sense of intimacy and draw others into the conversation.

- **Mirroring**: People are naturally drawn to those who make them feel understood and comfortable. **Mirroring** someone's body language, tone, and pace of speech can help build rapport and establish trust. For instance, if you notice someone leaning forward, you can subtly lean forward too. This helps to establish a subconscious connection and mutual understanding.

4. The Magic of Non-Verbal Presence

When you combine **eye contact, voice tone, and body language**, you create an undeniable sense of **presence**. A man who is aware of these non-verbal cues doesn't need to speak loudly or dominate a conversation to be noticed—he draws people in with his quiet assurance and unspoken charisma.

Imagine walking into a room. Your **body language** tells others if you're confident or anxious before you even say a word. When you **make eye contact** with someone, your presence immediately makes them feel seen and heard. When you speak with a well-modulated **voice tone**, your words resonate with power, authority, and authenticity. Together, these elements create an impression that lasts, influencing how others feel about you in a way that words alone cannot.

5. Practicing and Refining Your Non-Verbal Skills

Mastering these non-verbal communication tools takes practice, but the payoff is well worth the effort. You don't need to be perfect right away—start small, focus on one element at a time, and gradually incorporate it into your daily interactions.

- **Practice in front of a mirror**: Pay attention to your posture, eye contact, and gestures while speaking. Watch how your body language changes as you speak with confidence and clarity.

- **Record yourself speaking**: Sometimes, we don't realize how our voice sounds or how our body language comes across. Recording yourself speaking can help you identify areas to improve, like speaking too fast, not making enough eye contact, or slouching.

- **Get feedback**: Ask close friends or trusted mentors for feedback on how you come across in social settings. Honest feedback will help you refine your non-verbal communication even further.

Final Word: Non-Verbal Mastery is Charisma in Action

When you control **eye contact**, **voice tone**, and **body language**, you control how you're perceived in any social setting. Mastering these elements of communication is one of the most effective ways to build **charisma**, **confidence**, and **authentic connection**.

By paying attention to your non-verbal cues, you'll naturally command more respect and attention, creating an aura of **strength** and **magnetism** that others will find irresistible. You don't need to be the loudest person in the room to be noticed—sometimes, the most powerful person is the one who speaks the least but communicates the most with their presence.

Mastering Small Talk, Storytelling and Humor

In the realm of social dynamics, **small talk, storytelling**, and **humor** are the trifecta of charismatic communication. Mastering these elements will not only help you connect with others on a deeper level, but they'll also elevate your ability to engage and influence people in social situations. Whether you're navigating a networking event, a casual date, or a friendly get-together, these tools will make you feel at ease and ensure that others are drawn to you.

1. Small Talk: The Art of Breaking the Ice

Small talk is often underestimated, yet it is the cornerstone of all meaningful conversations. It's the initial bridge that helps you transition from surface-level interactions to something more substantial. While small talk may seem trivial, it's **essential for building rapport** and establishing a connection with others, especially when you don't know the person very well yet.

- **The Secret to Good Small Talk**: It's not about making profound statements or delivering clever one-liners. The key is being present, genuinely curious, and asking open-ended questions. By allowing the other person to share more about themselves, you make them feel important and heard, which naturally leads to a stronger connection.

- **Ask open-ended questions**: Instead of asking questions that can be answered with a simple "yes" or "no" (e.g., "Did you have a good weekend?"), ask questions that invite a more detailed response, like "What's the best thing that happened to you this weekend?" or "What do you love most about your job?" Open-ended questions show that you're genuinely interested in getting to know the other person.

- **Follow the flow**: Small talk is an exchange, not an interrogation. Listen actively and engage with what the other person is saying. Show interest by nodding, making eye contact, and offering a thoughtful response. This back-and-forth creates a natural flow that makes conversations feel effortless and enjoyable.

- **Don't be afraid of silence**: In the beginning, you might feel pressure to constantly fill the space with words. However, **silence can be powerful** if you let it be. A comfortable pause after a question or comment can allow both you and the other person to reflect and think. It also shows you're comfortable in your own skin, and not anxious about filling every moment with chatter.

2. Storytelling: Creating Connection Through Narrative

Humans are wired for stories. Our brains are naturally drawn to them because they make complex ideas easier to understand and more memorable. **Storytelling** is one of the most potent tools in your social arsenal. It can transform mundane conversations into engaging, emotionally resonant exchanges. Whether you're recounting an experience, sharing an anecdote, or illustrating a point, good storytelling can captivate your audience and make you more likable.

- **The Structure of a Good Story**: Great stories follow a simple structure: **setup, conflict, and resolution**. Start by painting a picture of the situation, introducing the characters, or setting the scene. Then, introduce a problem or challenge that creates tension. Finally, deliver the resolution in a way that wraps up the story with meaning or humor.

- **Use sensory details**: When telling a story, engage your audience by incorporating **sensory details**. Describe what you saw, heard, smelled, or felt in that moment. This brings the story to life and allows the listener to visualize the experience in their mind. For instance, instead of saying, "I went to the beach," you might say, "I was at the beach on a scorching day, the salty air mixing with the sound of crashing waves, and my feet sinking into the hot sand." The details make the story vivid and engaging.

- **Keep it relatable**: Great stories often center around universal themes— **overcoming challenges**, **moments of growth**, or **unexpected humor**. Make your stories relatable by tying them to common experiences or emotions. This helps create a bond with your listener because they can empathize with what you're sharing.

- **Add a personal twist**: When telling a story, the most powerful moments are often those where you reveal something **vulnerable** about yourself—whether it's a mistake you made, a lesson you learned, or an emotional insight. This vulnerability makes you human and gives your stories depth, allowing your listener to connect with you on a personal level.

3. Humor: The Ultimate Connector

Humor is one of the fastest ways to establish rapport, lighten the mood, and make others feel at ease. A well-timed joke or a funny anecdote can turn an awkward interaction into something memorable. However, humor is a skill that requires understanding timing, delivery, and the nuances of different social contexts. When used appropriately, it builds instant connection and shows that you don't take yourself too seriously.

- **The Power of Timing**: Humor is all about timing. A well-timed joke or witty comment can make even a simple statement feel more engaging. For example, a casual "I'm not saying I'm perfect, but I am close," delivered with a playful tone, can turn an otherwise normal conversation into something lighter and more enjoyable.

- **Self-deprecating humor**: One of the easiest ways to use humor is by laughing at yourself. **Self-deprecating humor** shows confidence because it demonstrates that you're not afraid to acknowledge your flaws or imperfections. This helps others feel comfortable around you, as it signals that you don't have a fragile ego. However, use this sparingly— too much self-deprecation can come across as insecurity.

- **Know your audience**: Different people find different things funny. What works with close friends might not work in a professional setting or with someone you're just getting to know. Be aware of the context and the other person's sense of humor. Avoid humor that could be seen as offensive or inappropriate, and stick to lighthearted, **non-controversial** jokes, especially in new or unfamiliar social environments.

- **Make use of observational humor**: Observational humor is about noticing the small, everyday things that everyone can relate to, like the awkwardness of waiting in a long line or the absurdity of a common situation. These kinds of observations often lead to humor that feels **authentic** and **relatable**. When you observe and comment on the quirks of the world around you, you invite others to see things from your perspective.

- **Avoid forced humor**: Humor should feel natural and unforced. If you try too hard to be funny, it can come across as desperate or uncomfortable. Let your humor flow organically from the conversation, and don't feel the need to be funny all the time. Sometimes, just a small, well-timed joke is enough to create connection.

4. Mastering the Flow: Combining Small Talk, Storytelling, and Humor

The real magic happens when you seamlessly blend small talk, storytelling, and humor. When you can move fluidly between these three, conversations become enjoyable, memorable, and meaningful. Here's how to combine them:

- Start with small talk to break the ice and establish rapport.

- Once you feel comfortable, transition into a **story** that naturally fits the conversation.

- Sprinkle in a touch of **humor** to keep the mood light and enjoyable, without overdoing it.

- Always be aware of the dynamics of the conversation. If someone else shares a story or joke, be sure to engage with it thoughtfully and add your own personal spin to keep the flow alive.

Final Word: The Art of Connection

Mastering small talk, storytelling, and humor is not about performing or impressing others. It's about **creating connection**. The more comfortable you become with these social tools, the more you'll be able to effortlessly engage with others, make lasting impressions, and build relationships.

These elements of communication allow you to showcase your **authentic self**, while creating space for others to do the same. The true charm of small talk, storytelling, and humor lies in their ability to transform ordinary interactions into extraordinary moments of connection.

How to Create Instant Connection Without Trying Too Hard

In social interactions, the most powerful connections often happen **effortlessly**, when you're not forcing anything. The trick to building an instant connection with someone is about **being present**, **authentic**, and **nonchalant**—a combination that exudes confidence without being overbearing. When you approach interactions with the mindset that you're not trying to impress anyone, you naturally give off an energy that others find magnetic and easy to connect with. Here's how to foster these kinds of effortless bonds.

1. Be Present: The Power of Full Attention

The key to creating an instant connection is being **fully present** in the moment. When you're truly engaged with the person in front of you, you're giving them the ultimate gift: your undivided attention. This doesn't mean just listening to what they say, but truly **attuning to their words**, **body language**, and even the **emotion** behind what they're sharing. People can tell when someone is distracted or only half-listening, and nothing kills connection faster than being mentally elsewhere.

- **Active listening**: When you engage with someone, make eye contact, nod occasionally, and use verbal affirmations like "I see," "That's interesting," or "Tell me more about that." These signals let the other person know you're deeply interested in what they're saying.

- **Mindfulness**: Clear your mind of distractions (the phone, personal worries) and focus entirely on the conversation. This creates a space where the other person feels truly valued, and naturally, they'll gravitate toward you.

- **Body language**: Your body language should mirror your level of engagement. Lean slightly forward to show interest, maintain good posture to signal confidence, and avoid crossing your arms or looking around the room, which can signal disinterest.

2. Share Vulnerability: Open Up and Be Real

People connect with **realness**. The more you allow yourself to be vulnerable—without oversharing or sounding rehearsed—the quicker you'll form a genuine bond. This doesn't mean you need to air your deepest secrets or get emotional in every conversation, but offering a glimpse into your authentic self fosters trust and emotional resonance.

- **Be authentic**: Don't try to be someone you're not. Whether it's your sense of humor, your personal opinions, or your quirks, embrace your true self. People are drawn to others who are confident in their individuality, and this can make an instant connection feel more natural.

- **Share personal stories**: Sharing an experience that's relevant to the conversation, or even a humorous anecdote, makes you seem approachable and relatable. Just make sure it's not about trying to impress—let it come out naturally and without expectation.

- **Don't overshare too early**: While vulnerability can create a deep connection, pacing is important. Share in small doses to avoid overwhelming the other person or coming across as trying too hard for sympathy or attention.

3. Use the Power of Empathy: Be Curious About Others

One of the easiest ways to create an instant connection is by showing genuine curiosity about the other person. People love to talk about themselves, but what makes it memorable is when you ask **thoughtful questions** that show you're not just going through the motions. When you express curiosity about someone's **thoughts**, **values**, and **experiences**, it shows that you value them as a unique individual, not just a source of conversation material.

- **Ask open-ended questions**: Questions that encourage someone to elaborate on their answers will give you a deeper understanding of who they are. For example, instead of asking "Do you like traveling?", ask "What's the best place you've ever traveled to and why?"

- **Practice active empathy**: When they share something personal or important to them, show empathy. Acknowledge their feelings, and let them know you understand their point of view. A simple "I can totally relate" or "That sounds like such a rewarding experience" goes a long way in building a connection.

- **Find common ground**: As they share their thoughts, look for areas where your experiences or interests overlap. Common ground creates an instant bond and gives you a sense of **shared understanding**.

4. Show Genuine Interest Without Overdoing It

Creating an instant connection isn't about bombarding the other person with a series of questions or anecdotes. It's about striking a balance between **engagement** and **allowing space** for the conversation to unfold naturally. The best connections happen when you're interested, but not overly eager.

- **Don't rush the conversation**: Allow the conversation to develop at its own pace. Instead of worrying about what to say next, focus on listening and reacting to what the other person is saying.

- **Give space for them to speak**: People appreciate when they feel **heard**. When you ask a question, allow them to fully answer without interrupting or hijacking the conversation to share your own story. This signals respect for their perspective.

- **Let things breathe**: Sometimes, the best way to create connection is through silence. Don't feel the need to fill every pause with chatter. Let the other person process their thoughts and respond in their own time.

5. Be Playful and Lighthearted

Humor and lightheartedness are great ways to create an instant connection because they break down barriers and help everyone feel more comfortable. Humor also has a way of making the interaction feel effortless, as it lightens the mood and helps people relax.

- **Make light observations**: Observational humor—like commenting on the quirky things around you or a funny situation—is a great way to ease tension and create an instant bond. Just keep it light and avoid anything that might offend.

- **Tease gently (without crossing boundaries)**: Playful teasing, when done in the right way, can create a fun, flirtatious dynamic. Keep the tone light and friendly, and make sure it's never at the expense of the other person's feelings. The goal is to **build rapport**, not to make anyone feel uncomfortable.

- **Don't force humor**: Humor should come naturally. If you try too hard to be funny or seem overly self-deprecating, it might come off as inauthentic. Let it happen organically.

6. Let Go of the Pressure to Impress

One of the most liberating aspects of creating connection without trying too hard is the realization that **you don't need to impress anyone**. When you free yourself from the pressure of performing or seeking approval, you automatically become more charismatic because your **confidence** and **comfort** shine through.

- **Stop overthinking**: Don't worry about saying the perfect thing or doing the right thing to impress someone. This kind of pressure can make you seem stiff or anxious. Relax, stay grounded, and trust that being your authentic self is more than enough to build a meaningful connection.

- **Focus on enjoyment**: Approach the conversation with the mindset of simply enjoying the interaction. When you're in a relaxed and fun headspace, your energy naturally draws people in.

Final Word: The Power of Ease and Authenticity

Creating instant connection is less about what you do and more about how you make the other person **feel**. The best connections are built on mutual respect, authenticity, and presence. When you're genuinely curious, empathetic, and willing to be yourself without trying to impress, others naturally gravitate toward you. And the more you practice this mindset of **effortless connection**, the easier it becomes to forge lasting, meaningful relationships—whether it's with strangers, friends, or potential partners.

Turning Rejection into a Weapon for Growth

Rejection is an inevitable part of life, especially when you're navigating the dating world, career pursuits, or personal goals. However, the way you perceive and respond to rejection determines whether it becomes a setback or a **powerful catalyst** for growth. While it's natural to feel disappointment, frustration, or even embarrassment when faced with rejection, it's important to realize that rejection isn't a reflection of your worth. Instead, it's an **opportunity** to evolve, refine your skills, and move closer to your goals. Here's how you can transform rejection into a weapon for your personal growth.

1. Shift Your Mindset: Rejection is Not Personal

The first step in turning rejection into growth is to **reframe your mindset** around it. Many people view rejection as a **personal attack**—believing that their value or identity is being questioned. This is a dangerous mindset that can lead to self-doubt, insecurity, and negative thought patterns.

- **Separate your actions from your identity**: When someone rejects you—whether it's a date, a job offer, or a personal project—understand that **rejection is about the situation, not you as a person**. For example, if someone turns down a date, it doesn't mean you're unworthy or unattractive. It simply means that **for whatever reason**, this specific situation didn't align. Your worth is inherent and untouched by any single rejection.

- **View rejection as feedback**: Rather than seeing rejection as a **failure**, treat it as a **learning experience**. Every time you face rejection, you're gaining valuable insights into what works and what doesn't. The key is to see rejection as **feedback**—it's not the end of the road, but an opportunity to adjust your approach and become better.

2. Use Rejection as a Mirror: Reflect and Improve

Rejection gives you the chance to **reflect** on your actions, your approach, and the decisions that led up to the rejection. Whether or not you can pinpoint exactly what went wrong, the process of introspection can help you improve moving forward.

- **Ask yourself constructive questions**: After a rejection, take some time to think about the situation. Did you communicate clearly? Were you confident and genuine, or did you try too hard to impress? Were there any red flags you ignored or signs you missed? By asking yourself these questions, you can pinpoint areas for improvement in your behavior, attitude, or strategies.

- **Learn from the experience**: Embrace rejection as an opportunity to **refine your skills**—whether that's your social skills, how you present yourself, or your emotional resilience. If you faced rejection in dating, maybe it's an opportunity to **work on building deeper connections** or refining your communication style. If it's career-related, it might be a signal to **upskill** in certain areas or adjust how you present yourself in interviews.

- **Identify patterns**: If you face repeated rejection in similar situations, take a step back and identify if there are recurring patterns. Maybe you're not being clear enough in your intentions, or perhaps you're projecting neediness or desperation without realizing it. Recognizing patterns gives you a roadmap for **changing habits** that may be hindering your success.

3. Build Resilience: Embrace the "Bounce-Back" Mentality

One of the most powerful outcomes of rejection is that it can **build emotional resilience**. Learning how to bounce back from setbacks is an essential skill for success in any area of life, and rejection is the perfect opportunity to cultivate this skill. How you handle rejection speaks volumes about your ability to persevere and adapt.

- **Don't dwell on the rejection**: It's easy to get caught in a spiral of self-pity, but **lingering on rejection** only strengthens its negative impact. Instead, **process the emotions**, but don't allow them to control you. Acknowledge your feelings, take a deep breath, and then refocus your energy on what's next.

- **Develop a growth-oriented mindset**: Instead of seeing rejection as a roadblock, view it as **part of the process**. Rejection isn't a reflection of your potential—it's simply a sign that there's a different path you need to take. With every "no" you encounter, you get closer to the "yes" you're seeking.

- **Strengthen your emotional toolkit**: Practice **emotional regulation** techniques such as mindfulness, journaling, or even speaking to a mentor or friend after rejection. The more resilient you become, the easier it will be to handle rejection in the future without it affecting your self-esteem or motivation.

4. Rejection Fuels Confidence and Persistence

When you embrace rejection and use it as a tool for growth, something extraordinary happens: you begin to build an **unstoppable confidence** that is rooted in **self-trust**. The more you face rejection without allowing it to deter you, the more you realize that **rejection isn't the end—it's just a stepping stone** on the path to success.

- **Confidence through experience**: The more rejection you experience and overcome, the more you realize that **it's a natural part of life**—and it no longer holds the power to break you. With each setback, you get stronger, more confident, and better equipped to handle the next challenge.

- **Embrace persistence**: Success rarely happens without a few setbacks. People who achieve great things—whether in dating, business, or life—are those who persist **in the face of rejection**. Rejection is simply the **universe's way of testing your commitment** to your goals. Those who keep going are the ones who eventually succeed, because they've learned to not take rejection personally, but instead use it as **fuel for growth**.

5. Shift the Focus: Rejection is Redirection

Often, rejection isn't a reflection of your value; it's simply the universe **redirecting you to something better**. Just because something didn't work out doesn't mean you've lost your chance. It might be the universe's way of saying, "This isn't the right fit for you," and guiding you toward something that's a more aligned opportunity.

- **See rejection as redirection**: Instead of seeing rejection as a closed door, look at it as an invitation to find a better one. If a job opportunity falls through or a romantic interest turns you down, don't view it as failure—see it as **the universe making space** for something better and more suited to your path.

- **Embrace the "next opportunity" mentality**: After facing rejection, **immediately** refocus your attention on the next opportunity. Whether it's another person, another job, or another chance, maintain the belief that the **right opportunities** are out there, and they are coming your way as long as you keep moving forward.

6. Turn Rejection Into Motivation for Action

Rather than allowing rejection to **discourage** you, use it to fuel **action**. Sometimes rejection can be a wake-up call to re-evaluate your approach and motivate you to **double down on your efforts**.

- **Use rejection as a challenge**: Take rejection as a challenge to do better next time. If you didn't get the job or the date you wanted, ask yourself, "How can I improve and come back stronger?" By shifting your mindset to treat rejection as a challenge, you keep yourself motivated to keep going.

- **Set new goals**: After facing rejection, use the energy of the moment to re-assess your goals. Maybe this rejection was a sign to refine your strategy, approach, or even your mindset. Take the lessons learned and use them to set new, **clearer goals** for the future.

Final Word: Rejection is Not Defeat—It's the Path to Mastery

Rejection is a natural part of any successful journey. Instead of viewing it as a defeat, **flip the script** and use it as an opportunity to grow, reflect, and persist. When you shift your mindset and embrace rejection as a weapon for growth, you'll develop the emotional strength, resilience, and confidence to navigate life's challenges with ease. Rejection doesn't define you; how you respond to it does. And if you can respond with grace, persistence, and self-awareness, you'll be on your way to mastering the art of growth and success.

7

Understanding High-Value Women

What Defines a High-Value Woman (and What Doesn't)

In the realm of dating and relationships, the term "high-value woman" often comes up—but what does it truly mean? It's essential to understand that the term is not about superficial traits or societal definitions of beauty or success. A high-value woman is not someone who is merely admired for her external appearance or wealth, but someone who embodies **inner strength**, **emotional intelligence**, **self-respect**, and **authenticity**. To truly understand what defines a high-value woman, it's important to also explore what **doesn't** define her.

What Defines a High-Value Woman?

1. Self-Respect and Boundaries

A high-value woman knows her worth and doesn't settle for less than she deserves. She has clear **boundaries** and doesn't compromise her values or standards for anyone. She's not afraid to say no, and she doesn't tolerate disrespect or mistreatment. This is a woman who understands that **self-respect** is non-negotiable. She doesn't seek validation from others; she knows who she is, and her sense of self is rooted in **confidence**, not external approval.

- **Boundaries with others**: She communicates clearly and confidently about her needs, whether it's in a romantic relationship, friendship, or work setting.

- **Self-worth over validation**: She doesn't need constant affirmation to feel valued, and she won't chase anyone who doesn't appreciate her.

2. Emotional Intelligence and Self-Awareness

A high-value woman is emotionally intelligent. She has a strong **awareness of her emotions,** and she understands how to manage them in a healthy, balanced way. She's comfortable with vulnerability, but she also knows how to regulate her reactions to avoid unnecessary drama or conflict. Her ability to communicate openly and honestly makes her a great partner, friend, and confidante.

- **Emotional regulation**: She understands how to stay calm under pressure and address challenges with composure.

- **Self-awareness**: She's in tune with her own thoughts and feelings, constantly striving for personal growth and emotional maturity.

3. Independence and Self-Sufficiency

A high-value woman doesn't rely on others for her happiness or well-being. She's independent in her pursuits, her finances, and her personal life. This independence doesn't mean she's emotionally distant or unapproachable—it simply means she's **self-sufficient** and values her personal growth and development. She is fully capable of standing on her own two feet, and she only invites others into her life who enhance her world, not define it.

- **Personal growth focus**: She's constantly evolving, whether it's in her career, education, fitness, or personal interests.

- **Healthy interdependence**: While she's independent, she's also open to sharing her life with someone who adds value, not someone who drains her energy or needs her to carry them.

4. Confidence, Not Arrogance

A high-value woman radiates **confidence**, but this confidence is rooted in her authentic self, not in an inflated sense of superiority. She doesn't need to boast about her accomplishments or talents, because her presence naturally commands respect. She knows her worth, and she doesn't need to prove it. Her confidence doesn't come from needing others to feel inferior, but from knowing she is complete in herself.

- **Humility paired with confidence**: She acknowledges her strengths without being boastful and owns her flaws without embarrassment.

- **Authentic self-assurance**: She is comfortable in her skin and doesn't rely on external factors like social media validation or comparison to others.

5. Authenticity and Integrity

A high-value woman values **authenticity** and is true to herself. She doesn't pretend to be someone she's not to please others. Her word is her bond, and she lives by a strong set of **integrity**. Whether she's at work, with friends, or in a relationship, she shows up as her true self, without putting on a facade.

- **Honesty and transparency**: She values honesty in all her relationships and expects the same in return.

- **Living by principles**: She holds strong to her values, and her actions align with her beliefs.

6. Kindness, Empathy, and Compassion

A high-value woman has a big heart. She is **kind**, **empathetic**, and **compassionate**, not just to those she loves, but to people in general. Her ability to understand and empathize with others is one of the qualities that make her magnetic. This doesn't mean she's a pushover—she still holds strong boundaries—but she values **kindness** and seeks to make the world a better place by spreading love and understanding wherever she goes.

- **Genuine empathy**: She can relate to others' feelings and offer support without judgment.

- **Acts of kindness**: Her kindness extends beyond just words—she shows it in her actions, helping others without expecting anything in return.

What Doesn't Define a High-Value Woman?

1. External Validation

A high-value woman doesn't base her worth on external **validation**—whether it's from a partner, family, or society. She doesn't need constant praise to feel good about herself. Her value is inherent and doesn't fluctuate with the opinions of others. She understands that self-worth comes from within, and she doesn't depend on others to tell her she's enough.

- **Not needing constant attention**: She doesn't seek attention or compliments just for the sake of it.

- **Not relying on others for self-esteem**: She doesn't base her self-worth on how others perceive her.

2. Toxic Traits Masked as Strength

Being a high-value woman isn't about being **"strong"** in the sense of being unyielding, controlling, or emotionally closed off. True strength lies in emotional intelligence, vulnerability, and adaptability—not in trying to dominate situations or relationships. High-value women don't resort to manipulative behaviors or put others down to feel powerful.

- **Not manipulative**: She doesn't use guilt, passive-aggressive behavior, or emotional manipulation to get what she wants.

- **Not emotionally closed off**: She's not afraid to be vulnerable and express her feelings, even when it's uncomfortable.

3. Superficial Traits or Materialism

A high-value woman isn't defined by her **appearance**, the car she drives, or the brand-name clothes she wears. While she might take care of herself and present herself well, she doesn't rely on material possessions or her looks to feel valuable or to seek approval. Her **inner qualities**—her character, intelligence, and emotional depth—are what truly define her.

- **Not defined by material wealth**: Her value is not in the things she owns or the status she holds.

- **Not obsessed with appearances**: She understands that beauty fades, but inner strength and integrity are lasting.

4. Neediness or Insecurity

A high-value woman is never **needy** or **insecure**. While it's normal to feel vulnerable at times, she doesn't depend on others to complete her or define her self-worth. She's comfortable being single and knows that the right person will come into her life when the time is right. Neediness, whether it's emotional or attention-seeking, is a trait she steers clear of because it undermines her sense of self-sufficiency and confidence.

- **Doesn't seek constant reassurance**: She doesn't require external validation to feel secure.

- **Not desperate for attention or love**: She doesn't chase after relationships for the sake of filling a void.

Final Word: The High-Value Woman Is an Inner State

A high-value woman is not about perfection or meeting society's superficial standards. She's a woman who has cultivated her **self-respect, emotional intelligence, authenticity**, and **strength** from within. She is the embodiment of a woman who knows her worth, holds healthy boundaries, and expects the same from others.

To understand what defines a high-value woman, think of her as a woman who is not afraid to live **true to herself**, to make her own decisions, to love deeply, and to prioritize her own growth and happiness. She is a woman who radiates confidence not because of how others see her, but because of how she sees herself. She is a woman who is not defined by external factors, but by the **depth** and **quality** of her character.

What She's Really Attracted to (Beyond Looks and Money)

In the world of dating, there's often a misconception that women are primarily attracted to a man's **physical appearance** or his **financial success**. While these aspects may catch her eye initially, they're not the real foundation for deep, lasting attraction. A high-value woman is looking for more than just a handsome face or a fat bank account. What truly captures her attention and ignites her desire is much deeper—and it has to do with **character**, **confidence**, and the **emotional connection** you can build together.

Here's what she's really attracted to, beyond just looks and money:

1. Emotional Intelligence and Depth

A high-value woman values a man who is emotionally intelligent—someone who is **self-aware**, **empathetic**, and capable of understanding and processing emotions. It's not enough for a man to be confident or strong on the outside; he needs to be **stable** and **aware** of his emotions on the inside.

- **Empathy and understanding**: A high-value woman appreciates a man who can **listen attentively** and understand her emotions without judgment. She doesn't need a man to solve her problems, but she does want someone who can support her emotionally and make her feel heard.

- **Self-regulation**: Emotional intelligence is about being able to control your reactions, especially in stressful or challenging situations. A high-value woman is attracted to a man who can maintain his composure and handle adversity with maturity and grace, rather than resorting to anger or defensiveness.

2. Confidence Without Arrogance

Confidence is one of the most magnetic traits in a man, but it's important to note that there's a fine line between **confidence** and **arrogance**. High-value women are attracted to men who exude a quiet confidence—those who know their worth, but don't feel the need to flaunt it or make others feel inferior. Confidence is not about boasting or needing constant validation—it's about **being comfortable in your own skin** and having the **courage to be authentic**.

- **Inner strength**: She's drawn to men who are **secure** in themselves and don't rely on external validation or praise to feel good. This type of confidence is often expressed through **assertiveness**, taking initiative, and being a leader in your own life.

- **Not trying to impress**: A high-value woman sees through men who try too hard to impress or prove their worth. Instead, she's attracted to men who are **genuine** and don't feel the need to impress her by showing off or putting on a façade.

3. Integrity and Authenticity

A high-value woman is highly attracted to a man who is genuine and operates with **integrity**. She wants someone who is true to their word, who lives by their values, and who shows up consistently, even when no one is watching. **Authenticity** is incredibly important—she appreciates men who aren't afraid to be themselves, regardless of what society or others might think.

- **Trustworthiness**: Integrity means doing the right thing, even when it's difficult. A high-value woman wants a man she can trust, someone who is **honest** and **transparent** in his actions, words, and intentions.

- **Being genuine**: She's attracted to men who can embrace their flaws, share their vulnerabilities, and show the real, unfiltered version of themselves, rather than presenting a perfect or curated image.

4. Ambition and Purpose

While financial success isn't the be-all and end-all, a high-value woman is certainly attracted to a man with **ambition** and a **sense of purpose**. This doesn't necessarily mean being the CEO of a company or having millions in the bank—it's about having a **drive** to succeed and an overarching vision for your life. A man who is on a **mission**, pursuing something meaningful, is incredibly attractive.

- **Focus on growth**: A high-value woman admires men who are constantly seeking **personal and professional growth**. Whether it's in their career, hobbies, or relationships, the key is that a man is continually **challenging himself** to be better and reach higher.

- **Purpose-driven**: She's attracted to men who are guided by a sense of purpose and direction, someone who knows what they want in life and is working towards it with **commitment** and **dedication**.

5. Strength, Stability, and Leadership

A high-value woman is often drawn to a man who has a natural sense of **leadership**—not necessarily in a traditional sense, but in his ability to **guide** and **support** others with **strength** and **stability**. She's not looking for someone who tries to control her or dominate situations, but rather someone who is **grounded** and confident in his ability to take charge when necessary.

- **Emotional stability**: Stability isn't just about finances—it's about **mental and emotional balance**. A high-value woman finds it attractive when a man can handle stress, challenges, and emotional turbulence with **level-headedness**.

- **Leadership through example**: She admires men who take responsibility for their actions and don't shy away from **leadership roles** in their personal and professional lives. A true leader inspires others through his actions and principles, not by forcing control.

6. Respect and Equality

A high-value woman is attracted to a man who treats her as an **equal**—someone who respects her autonomy, intelligence, and individuality. She values a partnership where there's mutual respect, where both people are committed to uplifting and supporting one another. **Respect** is the foundation of any great relationship, and she's looking for a man who values her as a partner, not an object or accessory.

- **Mutual admiration**: She seeks a relationship built on mutual **respect** and **understanding**, where both partners value and empower each other. It's not about being "above" or "below" the other; it's about supporting one another's growth and honoring each other's individuality.

- **Equality in decision-making**: She's looking for a partner who listens to her opinions, values her input, and makes decisions together, rather than simply dictating the course of their relationship or life.

7. Sense of Humor and Playfulness

A high-value woman is often attracted to a man who knows how to bring a sense of **humor** and **playfulness** to the relationship. Life is serious enough, and she appreciates a partner who can laugh, make her laugh, and create a **fun** atmosphere. The ability to laugh together—at life, at yourself, or even at the absurdity of everyday situations—can create a deep **emotional connection** and bring ease to difficult times.

- **Not taking life too seriously**: She wants a man who knows when to **lighten the mood** and not get bogged down by stress or negativity. A good sense of humor can be a great bonding tool.

- **Shared playfulness**: It's not just about making jokes—it's about being playful with one another, engaging in fun activities, and allowing the relationship to feel **dynamic** rather than static.

Final Word: It's About the Whole Package

While a high-value woman may appreciate a man who is attractive and successful, these superficial traits are never the whole picture. What really draws her in is the **depth of your character**, your ability to connect emotionally, and your ability to be a **stable, loving, and driven partner**. True attraction is built on **emotional intimacy**, **mutual respect**, and shared values—not on how much money you make or how good you look in a suit.

So, if you want to attract a high-value woman, focus on building your **inner strength**, becoming emotionally intelligent, being driven by a purpose, and showing her respect and kindness. When you show up as your **authentic self**, with a foundation of self-worth and integrity, the rest will naturally follow.

Red Flags to Watch for in Women (Yes, You Should be Picky)

When it comes to relationships, many men make the mistake of rushing in without paying attention to subtle (or sometimes glaring) warning signs that can signal deeper issues. While it's crucial to be open-minded and give people the benefit of the doubt, being selective and discerning in choosing a partner is essential to avoid unnecessary heartache down the road. You are not only investing your time but your emotional energy, your personal growth, and even your future. So, yes—you should absolutely be picky.

Being selective isn't about being critical or judgmental; it's about recognizing that **not every woman you meet is the right match for you**. Here are some key red flags that should make you think twice before getting deeply involved:

1. Lack of Emotional Maturity

Emotional maturity is one of the cornerstones of a successful, healthy relationship. If a woman is constantly throwing tantrums, blaming others for her problems, or unable to handle difficult situations without spiraling, it's a major red flag.

- **Signs of immaturity**: She plays emotional games (like testing you or creating drama), reacts impulsively, or avoids difficult conversations.

- **What to look for**: A high-value woman is capable of having difficult conversations, taking responsibility for her actions, and managing her emotions without projecting her issues onto you. She doesn't need you to constantly soothe or fix her emotional outbursts.

Why It Matters: A relationship with someone who isn't emotionally mature can quickly become exhausting, as you'll constantly be managing her emotional highs and lows instead of building a true partnership.

2. Manipulative Behavior or Gaslighting

One of the most toxic traits to watch for is manipulation—whether it's through **gaslighting**, guilt-tripping, or playing on your insecurities. A woman who uses tactics like these is often trying to control the narrative or gain power in the relationship. This can look like **making you doubt your own reality**, constantly putting you on the defensive, or shifting blame onto you when she's in the wrong.

- **Signs of manipulation**: She shifts blame, uses silent treatment to punish you, or makes you feel bad for setting boundaries. If you ever feel like you're walking on eggshells or constantly questioning your own perceptions, this is a major red flag.

- **What to look for**: A high-value woman values **honesty**, takes responsibility for her actions, and is open to constructive conversations. She doesn't play mind games to get her way.

Why It Matters: Manipulation is the foundation of a toxic relationship. If she is willing to manipulate you in small ways now, it will only get worse with time. Trust your instincts—being with someone who manipulates you will erode your self-worth and happiness.

3. Constantly Seeking External Validation

While it's natural to want appreciation and validation from your partner, someone who constantly seeks **external validation** from others (especially from other men) is a big red flag. If a woman's self-esteem is tied solely to what others think of her, it's a sign of insecurity that can create instability in the relationship.

- **Signs of external validation-seeking**: She regularly posts selfies or updates seeking compliments, and her self-worth fluctuates based on how much attention she gets. She may also talk about past relationships excessively or compare you to other men.

- **What to look for**: A high-value woman has **strong self-esteem** and is internally validated. She doesn't need constant affirmation from external sources to feel secure in herself or in the relationship.

Why It Matters: A woman who seeks constant attention from others can create feelings of insecurity and jealousy in the relationship. It's hard to build trust and intimacy with someone who doesn't fully respect and value what you have together.

4. She Disrespects Your Boundaries

Setting **boundaries** in a relationship is non-negotiable. Boundaries are about ensuring that both partners feel respected, valued, and safe. If a woman disrespects your boundaries—whether it's your time, your personal space, or your values—this is a significant red flag.

- **Signs of boundary disrespect**: She dismisses your feelings, pressures you to do things you're not comfortable with, or ignores your requests for space or time. She may also push for more commitment than you're ready for or try to manipulate you into doing things for her that go against your principles.

- **What to look for**: A high-value woman **respects** your boundaries and understands the importance of **mutual respect** in a relationship. She won't try to force you into doing things you're not ready for, and she values both her own and your needs.

Why It Matters: A relationship without boundaries is one in which control, manipulation, and resentment can easily take root. Healthy relationships are built on mutual respect for each other's individual needs and space.

5. She's Always the Victim

Everyone has struggles and challenges, but a woman who is **perpetually the victim** in every situation and never takes responsibility for her own actions can become emotionally draining over time. This can also indicate an inability to take accountability, which is essential for growth and maturity in a relationship.

- **Signs of victim mentality**: She frequently blames others for her problems, refuses to acknowledge her own shortcomings, and always expects others to rescue her. It's everyone else's fault, but never hers.

- **What to look for**: A high-value woman takes responsibility for her actions, acknowledges when she makes mistakes, and works to improve herself. She doesn't expect others to bear the brunt of her issues or constantly solve her problems.

Why It Matters: A woman who never takes accountability will drain your energy and create a lopsided, unbalanced relationship where you're constantly taking care of her emotional baggage. It's exhausting and unsustainable.

6. She's Too Focused on the Past

A woman who can't move on from her past—whether it's past relationships, trauma, or unresolved issues—can create emotional baggage that can weigh down the present and future of the relationship. While everyone has a history, it's important that she has **healed** and isn't dragging her emotional wounds into your relationship.

- **Signs of being stuck in the past**: She constantly talks about her exes, compares you to them, or hasn't processed previous emotional wounds. She may be overly cautious or guarded because of past experiences but never makes an effort to heal.

- **What to look for**: A high-value woman has **healed** from her past and doesn't let it dictate her current relationships. She's able to be present and focused on building something positive with you, rather than rehashing old wounds.

Why It Matters: A relationship that is stuck in the past can never grow. If she's still emotionally entangled with her past, it may prevent her from fully committing to you or your future together.

7. She's Overly Needy or Clingy

While it's natural for people to want affection and attention from their partners, a woman who is **overly needy** or **clingy** will often drain your energy and place unrealistic expectations on you. She may rely on you for her **happiness**, emotional stability, and sense of identity, which creates an unhealthy dynamic.

- **Signs of neediness**: She requires constant reassurance, demands your time and attention, and can't function without your validation. She may become overly jealous, possessive, or overly dependent.

- **What to look for**: A high-value woman is **secure** in herself and doesn't place the weight of her happiness solely on you. She is emotionally independent and doesn't demand more from you than is healthy for both of you.

Why It Matters: Neediness and dependency can create a toxic relationship dynamic, where you feel overwhelmed and suffocated. A healthy relationship should feel **empowering**, not draining.

Final Word: Trust Your Gut

At the end of the day, trust your instincts. If something feels off, it probably is. **Pay attention** to the red flags, and don't ignore them just because you're excited or feel pressured by the pace of the relationship. A high-value woman won't shy away from your standards or boundaries, and she will respect your need for a healthy, balanced relationship. By being discerning and aware, you not only protect your own well-being, but you also ensure that you're building a relationship with someone who is truly right for you in the long run.

Feminine Energy, Emotional Intelligence and Depth

Feminine energy is often misunderstood in modern times, with many viewing it as simply a reflection of beauty, softness, or emotional expression. While these elements are certainly part of it, feminine energy, in its true form, is much deeper and more powerful than meets the eye. It is an essential force that brings balance, creativity, empathy, and emotional intelligence to the dynamics of any relationship. A high-value woman embodies her feminine energy not as a performance, but as a deep, intrinsic part of her being.

In this section, we'll explore the interconnectedness of **feminine energy**, **emotional intelligence**, and **depth**—and why understanding these qualities is critical in recognizing the true value of a woman.

1. The Power of Feminine Energy

Feminine energy is not just about being nurturing or compassionate, although these qualities are important. It is, at its core, an energy of **receptivity**, **creativity**, and **empathy**. It is an energy that flows, nurtures, and connects. It complements masculine energy by bringing balance, intuition, and emotional depth to a relationship. Feminine energy can inspire growth, transform environments, and build strong, meaningful connections with those around her.

- **Receptivity**: A woman in her feminine energy is receptive to the world and to others. She doesn't need to force things; she trusts the process and flows with the rhythm of life. Her ability to **receive** is what allows her to be open and to foster meaningful connections—whether through love, friendships, or professional relationships.

- **Creativity**: Feminine energy is innately creative. It's the energy that births new ideas, art, and dreams. A high-value woman expresses her creativity in a multitude of ways—whether through her career, hobbies, or simply the way she engages with the world around her. It's her creativity that helps to keep relationships dynamic and interesting, constantly evolving and deepening.

- **Nurturing and Care**: While feminine energy is not confined to being nurturing, it plays a significant role in how a woman nurtures those she cares about. This doesn't just mean physical care; it's the **emotional support** and **compassionate attention** she offers to others. A woman with strong feminine energy knows how to create an environment of warmth and comfort, and she brings peace and serenity into her relationships.

2. Emotional Intelligence: The Heart of Feminine Energy

Emotional intelligence is the ability to recognize, understand, and manage our own emotions as well as the emotions of others. It's an essential quality in high-value women, and it is what allows them to connect on a deeper level with their partners, friends, and loved ones.

- **Self-Awareness**: A high-value woman with emotional intelligence is keenly aware of her emotions, triggers, and how they influence her behavior. She takes responsibility for her feelings and doesn't project them onto others. She is not driven by impulse but is capable of pausing to reflect on how she truly feels before responding to a situation.

- **Empathy**: Feminine energy is inherently empathetic. It is about feeling deeply for others, understanding their pain or joy, and offering the appropriate response. A woman with high emotional intelligence has the ability to listen and understand people's emotional needs without judgment. She creates an environment where others feel heard and seen.

- **Emotional Regulation**: Emotional intelligence isn't just about feeling deeply; it's also about managing emotions in a healthy and constructive way. A woman with emotional intelligence can navigate stress, conflicts, and frustrations with grace, avoiding outbursts or unnecessary drama. Instead of becoming overwhelmed by emotions, she can channel them in ways that strengthen relationships and promote understanding.

3. Depth: The Inner World of the Feminine

Feminine energy is deeply connected to the concept of **depth**—both intellectual and emotional. A high-value woman doesn't simply exist on the surface; she is a multi-dimensional being with a rich inner world that shapes her interactions, decisions, and the way she shows up in her relationships.

- **Intellectual Depth**: A woman in her full feminine energy is often curious, introspective, and invested in **personal growth**. She seeks to understand the world around her—not just superficially, but with a deep desire to uncover layers of meaning. She's well-read, thoughtful, and always exploring new ideas, perspectives, and philosophies. This intellectual depth enriches her conversations and allows her to connect on a more profound level with those around her.

- **Spiritual Depth**: In addition to intellectual pursuits, a high-value woman often has a spiritual depth, whether rooted in a particular belief system or a deep connection to nature, energy, or the universe. Her spirituality grounds her and provides her with a sense of **purpose**, guiding her decisions, relationships, and personal growth. This spiritual awareness allows her to offer wisdom and insight to those she loves.

- **Emotional Depth**: Feminine energy is closely linked to emotional depth. A high-value woman is someone who doesn't shy away from feeling deeply, but also has the maturity to process and learn from her emotions. She understands the value of vulnerability and sees it as a strength, not a weakness. Her emotional depth allows her to connect with others in a way that is raw, real, and truly transformative.

4. How Feminine Energy, Emotional Intelligence, and Depth Create Magnetic Attraction

Together, feminine energy, emotional intelligence, and depth form a potent combination that makes a woman incredibly magnetic and deeply attractive. The **balance** of these qualities draws people to her, creating an aura of both **warmth** and **mystery**. She has the ability to make those around her feel understood, valued, and supported while still retaining an air of intrigue and independence.

- **Authentic Connection**: Women who embody their feminine energy naturally attract men who are looking for a deep, authentic connection. They don't need to chase or manipulate—they simply draw people in with their genuine, open-hearted presence.

- **The Ability to Foster Growth**: Feminine energy is nurturing, but not in a way that stifles growth. It creates an environment where both partners can flourish. A high-value woman with emotional intelligence supports her partner's growth while also maintaining her own sense of identity and purpose. Her depth and empathy create a **safe space** for emotional intimacy, which allows the relationship to evolve and mature.

- **Balance with Masculine Energy**: When a man embraces his own masculine energy—his leadership, strength, and purpose—he complements the feminine energy of a high-value woman. Together, they create a harmonious dynamic where both energies thrive. The masculine provides structure and direction, while the feminine offers flow, intuition, and emotional richness. This balance creates an incredible **chemistry** and connection between partners.

Final Thoughts: The True Power of Feminine Energy

Feminine energy, emotional intelligence, and depth are some of the most powerful attributes a woman can possess. When she aligns with these qualities, she becomes a force of nature—magnetic, nurturing, and deeply connected to herself and others. A high-value woman understands that her true power comes from within: her ability to listen deeply, connect emotionally, and create an environment of growth and love.

For men who are seeking an authentic, fulfilling relationship, it's crucial to recognize the importance of these qualities. A woman who embodies these traits is not only emotionally intelligent but offers the depth and connection that can build the foundation for a strong, lasting relationship.

Creating Standards for the Women You Allow in Your Life

The women you allow into your life are a reflection of your standards, values, and ultimately, your self-worth. If you don't define and enforce these standards, you risk attracting women who don't align with your values or who might drain you emotionally, mentally, or even financially. Establishing clear, non-negotiable standards isn't about being rigid or judgmental—it's about creating a healthy environment where you can thrive and form meaningful, lasting relationships.

In this section, we'll explore the importance of setting standards, what these standards should include, and how to maintain them while building healthy connections with women.

1. Why Standards Are Essential

Setting standards for the women you allow in your life is not just about finding the "right" partner—it's about **honoring yourself**. Standards are a way of protecting your time, energy, and emotional investment. They serve as a **barrier** against negative influences and ensure that you attract women who truly add value to your life, not detract from it.

Having high standards communicates to the world that you value yourself and are unwilling to settle for anything less than the best. It signals that you are **self-aware**, have a clear vision of what you want, and are committed to creating a life that aligns with your values. It's also about respecting your future: by choosing the right women, you're investing in a partnership that has the potential to support your growth and elevate both of your lives.

2. Defining Your Standards: What to Look for

Your standards should be based on **core principles**—the qualities and values that matter most to you in a partner. These are personal to you, and they should reflect who you are, what you need, and what you aspire to be. While everyone's standards will differ, here are some essential qualities you should consider when defining your standards:

- **Emotional Maturity**: You want a woman who is emotionally mature— someone who takes responsibility for her actions and emotions and is capable of having meaningful conversations. She shouldn't resort to emotional manipulation, dramatic outbursts, or avoid difficult discussions. A woman with emotional maturity can regulate her emotions and manage conflict in a healthy way.

- **Respect for Yourself and Others**: Respect is one of the most important foundations of any relationship. A woman who respects you will value your time, your opinions, and your boundaries. She will also show kindness and respect to others, especially in challenging situations. If she disrespects others—whether it's family, friends, or even strangers—there's a good chance that respect for you will wane as well.

- **Ambition and Drive**: A high-value woman is **driven** and **purposeful**. She has her own goals, passions, and vision for the future. She's not looking to rely on you for validation or a sense of purpose. Instead, she's independent and seeks someone who can complement her journey, not complete it. A woman with ambition will inspire you to level up in your own life, and together, you'll create a strong, dynamic partnership.

- **Physical and Mental Health**: Take stock of the health standards you want in a partner. This includes **physical health**, such as maintaining a fit and healthy lifestyle, as well as **mental health**, such as emotional stability, self-awareness, and maturity. While everyone has their challenges, a high-value woman is generally someone who takes care of her body and mind—because she knows that self-care is foundational to living a fulfilling life.

- **Authenticity and Integrity**: One of the most important qualities to look for in any partner is authenticity. A woman who is real and true to herself will be transparent, honest, and trustworthy. You want someone who doesn't hide behind masks, put on airs, or live a double life. **Integrity**—doing what is right even when no one is watching—should be a cornerstone of her character. A relationship based on authenticity creates trust, and trust is essential for building a deep connection.

- **Shared Values**: Ensure your values align with hers. This could include how you both approach **family**, **money**, **religion**, or **personal development**. Differences in core values can be a source of major conflict over time, so it's essential to be clear about your fundamental beliefs and ensure she shares or respects them.

- **Feminine Energy and Emotional Intelligence**: While each person has a combination of masculine and feminine traits, it's important that a woman has a healthy balance of **feminine energy** and **emotional intelligence**. She should be emotionally aware, capable of expressing vulnerability when appropriate, and able to create a connection based on mutual understanding. This doesn't mean she should be passive or overly dependent, but rather that she can nurture, care for, and emotionally support the relationship.

3. How to Maintain Your Standards

Setting standards is just the first step—the real work comes in maintaining them. To attract and keep the women who align with your values, you must consistently enforce your standards. This is where many men falter. It's easy to get excited and lower your standards when you feel pressure or when a woman seems "perfect" in the moment. But lowering your standards is a surefire way to invite chaos and instability into your life. Here's how to maintain your standards:

- **Don't Settle for Less**: The moment you compromise on your standards, you are setting yourself up for dissatisfaction and resentment. If you meet someone who doesn't meet your core values or emotional needs, don't settle out of convenience, loneliness, or pressure. It's better to remain single and focused on your growth than to get involved with someone who doesn't align with your values.

- **Enforce Boundaries Early**: Boundaries are a form of self-respect, and when you clearly communicate your boundaries from the beginning of a relationship, you set the tone for how you expect to be treated. Be firm about your non-negotiables—whether they are about respect, communication, or personal space—and don't back down if those boundaries are crossed.

- **Don't Fear Loss**: It's natural to fear losing someone, but it's even worse to fear losing yourself. If a woman doesn't respect your standards, let her go. You deserve someone who complements you—not someone who takes you off course or pulls you into unhealthy dynamics. Trust that the right person will come along when you remain true to your values.

- **Observe, Don't Just Listen**: Actions speak louder than words. Pay attention to how a woman behaves over time, not just how she presents herself in the early stages of dating. Does she follow through on her promises? Does she respect your time, space, and emotions? Look for consistency in her behavior rather than getting caught up in fleeting moments of charm.

- **Be Willing to Walk Away**: If, over time, you see that your standards are not being met, don't be afraid to walk away. You will always be better off alone than with someone who isn't the right fit for you. The strength to walk away when necessary is a powerful expression of self-respect and personal integrity.

4. The Impact of Your Standards

When you create and enforce high standards for the women you allow into your life, you are not only improving your own life but also raising the standard of the women you attract. A high-value man who values himself will naturally attract women who also value themselves. The energy you put out into the world determines the type of energy you attract.

By establishing strong, non-negotiable standards, you will create a life filled with quality relationships, mutual respect, and a foundation for growth—both as individuals and as a couple. These standards will help you avoid unhealthy dynamics and ensure that every relationship you engage in is a source of empowerment, not depletion.

Final Thoughts: Embrace Your Worth

At the core of creating standards is the understanding of **your own worth**. When you know and value yourself, you won't tolerate anything less than respect, love, and alignment with your principles. By setting and maintaining high standards, you send a powerful message to the world that you are not only worthy of love and respect, but that you are committed to attracting the best, most aligned partners into your life.

8

Dating with Purpose – Strategy Over Game

The Difference Between Chasing and Attracting

In the world of dating, there is a crucial distinction that every man must understand if he's going to build lasting, meaningful relationships: **the difference between chasing and attracting**. This difference isn't just about how you approach women—it's about how you perceive your own value, the role you play in relationships, and the mindset you adopt. Chasing leads to frustration, dependence, and a lack of fulfilment, while attracting leads to mutual respect, desire, and a dynamic partnership based on attraction rather than need.

In this section, we'll dive deep into what it means to **chase** versus to **attract**, and why shifting your mindset is essential for creating purposeful, successful relationships.

1. Chasing: The Trap of Neediness

Chasing is often driven by **neediness**—the idea that you must pursue, prove yourself, or "win" the affection of a woman. This behavior typically arises when you are focused more on the **outcome** (getting the girl, having the relationship) than on the **process** (developing yourself, building genuine connections). The problem with chasing is that it creates a **power imbalance**. When you chase, you're in a reactive position, constantly looking for signs of approval and validation. You may find yourself:

- **Pushing for Validation**: When you chase, you seek external validation to feel good about yourself. You may constantly ask for reassurance, make grand gestures to win approval, or try to change who you are to fit the woman's ideal. This need for external validation can leave you feeling empty and unfulfilled, no matter how much attention or affection you receive.

- **Over-Pursuing**: Chasing often leads to over-pursuit. You send constant texts, make frequent calls, or initiate most conversations, hoping that this will create a connection. This can make you appear desperate or overly eager, pushing the woman away rather than drawing her in. The reality is that most high-value women are turned off by neediness and lack of self-assurance.

- **Being Reactive Rather Than Proactive**: Chasing leads to a reactive stance. You're responding to what the woman is doing or not doing, and your actions are dictated by her behavior rather than your own desires or intentions. This reactive mindset leaves you constantly guessing and doubting, creating an unstable and unbalanced dynamic in the relationship.

- **Losing Your Sense of Self**: When you chase, you often compromise your own needs, interests, and boundaries in order to gain her approval. Over time, this can lead to **resentment** and **frustration**, as you realize that you've been giving more of yourself than you've been receiving in return.

2. Attracting: The Power of Presence and Value

Attracting, on the other hand, is about embodying your **best self**, showing up with confidence, and letting women be drawn to who you are naturally. Attraction is a **magnetic force**—it's not something you have to chase or force. It's about creating an environment where your **presence**, **values**, and **purpose** draw the right people to you, effortlessly. Here's what it means to attract instead of chase:

- **Self-Assurance and Confidence**: When you focus on attracting, you are grounded in your own worth. You know that you don't need to chase anyone to validate your existence. You've worked on becoming a man of **value**—physically, emotionally, mentally, and spiritually—and you bring that energy into every interaction. Your confidence comes from within, and it radiates outward, making you naturally attractive without having to work hard at it.

- **The Power of Choice**: When you're attracting, you know that women are not the only prize in the relationship. You're not seeking approval from anyone because you've already validated yourself. You have standards and boundaries, and you're aware that not every woman is right for you. This self-respect and selectiveness naturally attract the women who share your values and are genuinely interested in you for who you are.

- **Being Present, Not Desperate**: Attraction is rooted in **presence**. When you stop chasing, you start to show up fully in the moment. You listen attentively, engage authentically, and offer value in every interaction. You don't rush, and you don't chase after what's not aligned with your purpose. You are patient, knowing that when you embody your true self, the right connections will follow.

- **High-Value Interactions**: When you attract, the relationships you form are **mutual**. Women are drawn to your energy, not your efforts. They are excited to pursue you as much as you are them. This creates an environment of **balance** and **respect**, where both parties are fully invested in the connection and growth of the relationship.

- **Having a Full Life**: Attracting doesn't require constant attention or effort—it requires that you have a life that's already fulfilling. You're busy with your goals, passions, career, and hobbies. You're not waiting around for someone to complete you, because you are already **whole**. Women are naturally attracted to men who are confident, independent, and have a strong sense of purpose. When you're living a full, exciting life, women will want to be a part of it.

3. Why Chasing Leads to Frustration, and Attracting Leads to Fulfilment

The key difference between chasing and attracting lies in the **energy** you bring to the table. When you chase, you're giving off a **desperate** energy, one that comes from a place of **lack**. You feel as though you need her validation to feel good about yourself. This creates a power imbalance and a dynamic where the woman is more likely to pull away because she can sense the desperation.

Attracting, on the other hand, comes from a place of **abundance** and **self-sufficiency**. You know your worth and are not seeking external validation. Women sense this energy and are naturally drawn to it because it exudes strength, confidence, and purpose. When you focus on attracting, you create a partnership built on mutual desire and respect, not one where you feel like you're constantly fighting for attention or affection.

The irony is that the more you chase, the more you push people (especially women) away. The more you focus on becoming your best self and living a life that aligns with your purpose, the more attractive you become—not just to women, but to the world around you.

4. The Practical Shift: How to Move from Chasing to Attracting

Shifting from a mindset of chasing to one of attracting takes time, self-awareness, and conscious effort. Here's how to make that shift:

- **Focus on Your Own Growth**: Make sure you're growing as a man—not just for the sake of attracting women, but for your own fulfilment. Work on your career, health, hobbies, and social life. When you're constantly evolving and improving yourself, your energy becomes magnetic.

- **Cultivate Confidence**: Confidence is attractive, and the only way to build it is through consistent self-work. Take care of your body, learn new skills, set and achieve goals, and constantly expand your horizons. A man who is confident doesn't need to chase validation; he knows he's already worthy.

- **Create Boundaries and Standards**: Women can sense your level of self-respect through your boundaries and standards. Define what you will and won't tolerate in relationships and ensure that you're attracting women who align with your values. A man who knows his worth and has boundaries will naturally attract women who respect him.

- **Be Patient**: Attraction doesn't happen overnight. It's a natural, organic process that takes time. Be patient with yourself and with the women you meet. Focus on enjoying the process of building connections rather than rushing for an outcome.

- **Embrace Abundance**: When you realize that you are not limited to any one woman, you free yourself from the desperation of chasing. You understand that there are plenty of opportunities and that you don't have to settle for anything less than what you deserve.

Final Thoughts: Attraction is a Mindset

Ultimately, the difference between chasing and attracting is a matter of mindset. When you are focused on becoming the best version of yourself and living a full, meaningful life, you'll find that you don't need to chase anyone. Instead, people—including women—will naturally be drawn to you. **Attraction** comes from self-love, confidence, and purpose, not from external validation. Shift your focus from pursuing others to building your own life, and watch as women are drawn to the strong, confident man you're becoming.

How to Vet Women without Losing Your Power

When you are dating with purpose and striving to build meaningful connections, it's essential to be selective about the women you invite into your life. **Vetting** women is a necessary step in ensuring you invest your time and energy into relationships that align with your values and goals. However, there's a fine line between being discerning and losing your power in the process. If you're not careful, you may find yourself compromising your standards or becoming overly invested in a woman before you've fully assessed whether she's the right fit for you.

In this section, we'll discuss how to effectively vet women while maintaining your sense of self-worth, emotional independence, and masculine power. This approach ensures that you don't just attract the right women but also build relationships that are healthy, balanced, and empowering for both parties.

1. Understand Your Own Standards First

Before you can vet a woman effectively, you need to have a clear understanding of your **own values, needs, and boundaries**. This means defining what you truly want in a partner—what qualities are essential for you to feel fulfilled and respected in a relationship.

- **Clarity is Power**: Take the time to reflect on your personal values, life goals, and the kind of woman you want to be with. Do you want someone who shares your passion for personal growth? A woman who is emotionally mature, independent, and goal-driven? Define these characteristics in advance, so you're not swayed by superficial traits or temporary emotions.

- **Create Non-Negotiables**: These are qualities or behaviors that you simply will not tolerate in a partner—things like dishonesty, disrespect, or a lack of emotional intelligence. Once you've established your non-negotiables, you can filter potential partners through these criteria without losing your power or compromising on what truly matters.

2. Maintain Emotional Detachment

One of the biggest mistakes men make when dating is becoming emotionally attached too early in the process. Emotional attachment, especially when it's based on chemistry or superficial attraction, can cloud your judgment and cause you to overlook red flags.

- **Date with Objectivity**: Keep your emotions in check during the vetting phase. This doesn't mean being cold or distant, but rather being able to evaluate her actions and behavior objectively. Observe how she treats others, how she communicates, and whether her actions align with her words. Emotional detachment allows you to see the relationship from a clearer perspective and helps you avoid being swept up in temporary feelings.

- **Take Your Time**: There's no rush. Whether it's a few weeks or a few months, take your time to really get to know her before making any emotional commitments. The best relationships are built on **slow, organic growth**. When you take the time to assess someone's true character, you prevent yourself from losing your power in the excitement of early attraction.

3. Assess Her Actions, Not Just Her Words

Words are easy to say, but actions reveal the true nature of a person. In the early stages of dating, women will often say things to make a good impression, but it's their **consistent behavior** over time that will tell you whether they're a good match.

- **Look for Consistency**: Pay attention to how she behaves in different situations. Does she treat waitstaff with respect? Is she reliable and follow through on her commitments? Does she show empathy and consideration for others? A woman who consistently demonstrates integrity and kindness is far more likely to be a good fit than someone who only says the right things when it benefits her.

- **Observe Her Boundaries**: A woman who respects your boundaries will naturally expect the same from you. Take note of how she responds to yours. If she pressures you into doing things you're not comfortable with or consistently disrespects your limits, that's a red flag. Healthy relationships are built on mutual respect for each other's boundaries.

- **Notice Her Emotional Stability**: Women who display emotional volatility, constant drama, or inability to manage conflict in a healthy way should be vetted carefully. Emotional maturity is key to a stable and thriving relationship. Pay attention to how she handles stress, conflict, and disappointment. Does she handle situations calmly and with composure, or does she react impulsively and emotionally?

4. Be Assertive, Not Passive

Vetting women requires you to take an active role in the process. You can't afford to sit back and wait for someone to prove their worth to you. Being assertive means communicating your needs, values, and expectations clearly, without being aggressive or overly controlling. This helps maintain your power while also ensuring you're attracting women who align with your standards.

- **Ask the Right Questions**: Don't be afraid to ask meaningful questions that reveal her character and intentions. These questions should align with your core values, such as her outlook on relationships, how she views personal growth, or how she handles conflict. The goal is to gauge whether she is compatible with your lifestyle and life goals.

- **Don't Be Afraid to Walk Away**: If at any point during the vetting process you feel like a woman is not meeting your standards, trust your gut and be willing to walk away. This is a powerful act of self-respect. Women are naturally attracted to men who have the courage to set and enforce boundaries. If you cling to someone who isn't right for you, you lose your power and invite unnecessary drama into your life.

5. Gauge Her Level of Investment

A balanced relationship requires **mutual investment**—emotional, mental, and physical. During the vetting process, observe how much she is investing in the relationship. Are the interactions one-sided? Does she put effort into making plans, initiating communication, or showing interest in your life?

- **Look for Reciprocity**: Healthy relationships are based on mutual effort. While it's normal for one person to initiate sometimes, both partners should take turns investing in the relationship. If you're doing all the work, you may be in a dynamic where you're giving more than you're receiving, which can be draining in the long term.

- **Respect for Your Time and Energy**: Does she value your time and energy? If she is consistently late, cancels plans without valid reasons, or shows signs of emotional unavailability, it may be a sign that she is not as invested as you are. Be mindful of these signs and don't be afraid to set boundaries around how you allow others to treat your time.

6. Stay Grounded in Your Own Life

Vetting women doesn't mean losing sight of your own life, goals, and purpose. In fact, the more grounded and focused you are on your own mission, the easier it becomes to identify women who genuinely align with your life rather than those who may be simply looking to distract or complicate it.

- **Keep Your Own Interests and Activities**: Make sure that dating does not overshadow your personal growth, career, and hobbies. When you maintain a strong sense of self and continue pursuing your own passions, you'll attract women who appreciate your ambition and drive, rather than those who seek to fill a void in your life.

- **Remain Independent**: The more emotionally independent you are, the less you will rely on the validation or approval of women. This gives you a **massive advantage** during the vetting process because you are able to assess her qualities objectively, without being influenced by the need to be validated or liked.

Final Thoughts: Stay in Your Power

Vetting women is not about playing games or treating people as "projects." It's about understanding your own value and making conscious decisions about who you allow into your life. By staying grounded in your standards, emotional detachment, and self-respect, you'll be able to make better choices in your dating life without losing your power.

Remember, the goal is not just to find a woman—but to find a **high-value woman** who complements your life and elevates both of you. By approaching dating with a clear mindset and purpose, you empower yourself to attract women who are aligned with your values and contribute to a meaningful, lasting relationship.

First Dates that Set the Right Frame

The first date is your opportunity to **set the tone** for the type of relationship you want to build. It's not just about impressing her or having a good time—it's about establishing the **frame** for the dynamic between you both. The frame is the **emotional and psychological space** that you create, and it shapes how the date progresses and how you are perceived. A strong, masculine frame ensures that you're in control of the interaction without coming off as domineering or rigid. It's about confidently guiding the date, while also being mindful of her energy, needs, and boundaries.

In this section, we'll explore how to set the right frame from the moment you walk into that restaurant or meet for coffee. A well-set frame allows you to express your values and intentions clearly, while also creating an atmosphere where both of you can connect authentically and comfortably.

1. Set the Tone with Confidence and Leadership

From the moment you meet her, you want to demonstrate that you're a man who knows what he's doing. Confidence isn't about being arrogant or overbearing—it's about **being comfortable in your own skin** and taking the lead in a respectful, natural way. Women are drawn to men who project confidence, because it signals strength, reliability, and the ability to create stability in uncertain situations.

- **Lead with Your Presence**: When you first meet, make sure to greet her with **eye contact** and a warm but firm handshake. Your body language should be open and relaxed, signaling that you are comfortable and in control of yourself. Stand tall, shoulders back, and maintain good posture throughout the date. Your presence should feel grounded and calm—this is the essence of setting a strong masculine frame.

- **Take the Lead in Conversation**: While it's important to listen actively and engage with what she says, don't let the conversation drag on without direction. Take the lead by introducing topics, guiding the flow of the discussion, and ensuring that the conversation doesn't get stuck in a dull or awkward loop. Ask open-ended questions that encourage her to share about herself, but don't let her dominate the conversation. **Assertiveness** in conversation signals that you're not afraid to take charge, but are also genuinely interested in her thoughts and feelings.

- **Stay Calm Under Pressure**: The first date may come with its share of awkward moments—whether it's an uncomfortable silence or a minor mishap. How you react to these situations is crucial. Instead of panicking or trying to fill every moment with forced chatter, stay calm and composed. **Emotional control** is a key element of a strong frame, and it allows you to handle any curveballs that come your way with grace and confidence.

2. Keep the Date Fun, Light, and Engaging

While you want to set a strong frame, it's equally important to ensure the date remains enjoyable and engaging. If the atmosphere is too stiff or serious, it can cause tension and discomfort. A successful first date balances **playfulness** with meaningful connection.

- **Avoid Heavy Topics Early On**: The first date isn't the time to dive into deep, heavy conversations about politics, religion, or controversial topics. Instead, focus on lighter, more engaging discussions—ask about her interests, hobbies, travel experiences, and what excites her. Keep things fun and light-hearted while still showing genuine curiosity about her life and passions.

- **Create a Playful, Fun Environment**: A strong masculine frame doesn't mean being overly serious. Show that you can have fun and make her laugh. Light teasing, playful banter, and spontaneous moments of humor can create a connection that feels easy and natural. But be careful not to cross into **mockery** or anything that could be seen as insulting. Playfulness shows that you're confident enough to not take things too seriously, and that you can bring out the best in her.

- **Be Attentive and Present**: While fun is important, don't forget to be attentive. Put away your phone, make her feel like she has your full attention, and ensure that you're present in the moment. Being genuinely interested and engaged in her company is one of the easiest ways to build connection and rapport. She'll appreciate the fact that you're not distracted and are focused on making her feel valued.

3. Maintain Your Masculine Frame Without Overpowering Her

One of the biggest mistakes men make on first dates is being **too passive** or, on the flip side, being **too dominating**. It's important to find a balance where you're confident and assertive but also respectful of her space, autonomy, and needs. The right frame is one of **mutual respect**, where you lead without trying to control or overwhelm her.

- **Set the Pace**: As the man, you want to take the lead in setting the pace for the date—this includes choosing the venue, controlling the timing, and keeping the flow of the interaction on track. Don't let her dictate the date entirely, but also be open to her preferences and input. You don't want to seem rigid or inflexible, but neither should you give away all the control.

- **Be Mindful of Her Comfort**: A big part of maintaining the right frame is being aware of her comfort zone. **Watch her body language**—is she leaning in, making eye contact, and smiling, or is she pulling back, avoiding eye contact, or fidgeting? These are subtle cues that tell you whether she's enjoying herself and feeling comfortable. If you sense that she's pulling away, give her space. Acknowledge her boundaries without being defensive or anxious.

- **Don't Chase Validation**: One of the quickest ways to lose your masculine frame is to seek constant validation. Don't fish for compliments, constantly reassure her, or act overly eager to impress her. While you do want to show interest, **be content with the knowledge that you are enough as you are**. A man who doesn't need validation sends a powerful message that he's comfortable in his own skin and doesn't rely on others to define his self-worth.

4. Build Trust Through Subtle Signals

A key element of the masculine frame is the ability to build **trust and safety** without forcefully pushing for intimacy. It's crucial that you signal your intentions subtly—making it clear that you're a man who values **mutual respect** and is interested in building something meaningful, without rushing the process.

- **Be Honest and Transparent**: While you don't need to overshare your life story, it's important to be honest about who you are and what you want. If you're looking for a long-term relationship, don't be afraid to hint at it in a subtle way without coming on too strong. Share your values, goals, and what's important to you in life. This signals to her that you have clarity and direction, which is attractive and builds trust.

- **Create Emotional Safety**: The best way to set the right frame is to create a space where both of you can be comfortable and open with each other. Be genuinely interested in her, listen actively, and show empathy when needed. This builds trust without overtly trying to do so. When she feels emotionally safe with you, she will be more likely to open up, which sets the foundation for a deeper connection.

- **Physical Touch with Caution**: Physical touch is an important aspect of building intimacy, but it should be done gradually and with respect. A light touch on the arm or a gentle hand on her back can signal your interest, but don't force it. If she reciprocates the physicality, you can naturally escalate. Always make sure your actions are respectful of her boundaries, and let her comfort level guide the pace.

5. Leave Her Wanting More

One of the keys to maintaining a strong frame is to end the date on a high note, leaving her wanting more rather than overstaying your welcome. **Create an air of mystery** and don't reveal everything about yourself or your intentions right away.

- **Don't Overstay Your Welcome**: As the date progresses, gauge how well it's going. If things are going well, consider wrapping things up while the mood is still positive. Avoid the temptation to linger too long and risk the date dragging on. Leaving the date early enough that she feels like there's still more to explore can spark curiosity and anticipation for the next meeting.

- **End with Clear Intentions**: As you part ways, make sure to communicate your intentions clearly. If you had a great time and want to see her again, express that, but do so confidently and without pleading. A simple, "I had a great time tonight. I'd love to do this again soon," is all you need to leave the right impression.

Final Thoughts: Your Frame is the Foundation of Attraction

Setting the right frame on a first date is crucial for establishing the kind of relationship you want. By maintaining confidence, leadership, and emotional control, while also being attentive, respectful, and genuine, you create an atmosphere where both of you can connect authentically. The right frame builds a sense of safety, respect, and attraction, making it clear that you are a man who knows his value and is not afraid to lead, but also open to genuine connection.

Remember: the first date isn't just about impressing her—it's about showing up as your best self and making sure that the dynamic is set in a way that works for both of you. When you set the right frame, you're not only positioning yourself for success in that moment but also laying the groundwork for a relationship built on mutual respect, attraction, and authenticity.

Keeping Momentum Without Playing Games

In the world of dating and relationships, there's a lot of talk about **playing games**—strategies to appear more attractive, creating mystery, or even manipulating emotions to keep someone on their toes. While these tactics might work temporarily or in certain situations, they undermine authentic connections and rarely lead to long-term, fulfilling relationships. Instead, true attraction and lasting connection come from maintaining **genuine momentum**, where both partners are moving forward naturally and intentionally without resorting to games or manipulation.

In this section, we'll explore how to keep the momentum of a relationship or dating dynamic growing, without falling into the trap of playing games or relying on shallow tactics. The key is to focus on building a meaningful connection based on mutual respect, clear communication, and alignment of values, rather than tricks and psychological manipulation.

1. Be Consistent Without Over-Communicating

The first step in keeping momentum without playing games is to be **consistent** in your behavior and communication. People naturally want to feel secure in their connections, so inconsistency can create confusion or anxiety. However, **consistency** does not mean overwhelming her with constant texts or calls. It's about striking the right balance between staying engaged and giving her the space to miss you.

- **Texting and Calling with Intent**: Rather than sending a flurry of messages just to stay "top of mind," reach out with intention. Share things that genuinely matter to you or offer insight into your day-to-day life, but avoid over-texting for the sake of attention. When you do communicate, make sure your messages are thoughtful and show interest in her, rather than just filling space.

- **Don't Overcompensate**: Sometimes, when we feel the pressure to keep things moving, we can overcompensate by becoming overly available or constantly texting. This approach, while seemingly flattering, can come off as needy and put unnecessary pressure on the other person. **Quality over quantity** is the key. Make your communication meaningful, and leave room for her to reciprocate and show interest.

- **Give Her Space**: You don't need to be in constant communication to maintain momentum. In fact, giving her space to process her own thoughts and feelings is a vital part of keeping things natural. If you see her pulling back, don't chase after her. Let her come to you in her own time, which fosters a sense of intrigue and keeps the dynamic grounded in mutual desire.

2. Be Honest and Transparent About Intentions

Keeping momentum alive requires both of you to feel like the relationship is progressing in a way that meets each other's needs. Playing games often involves creating **uncertainty** about where things stand, but that only breeds confusion and can derail the connection. Instead, the key is to be honest and transparent about your intentions, without being overly rigid or forcing outcomes.

- **Express Your Intentions Clearly**: While you don't need to spell out everything immediately, being clear about your intentions is vital. If you're dating with purpose, make sure your actions and words align. If you're interested in something more serious, express it in a way that's respectful of her pace. Avoid sending mixed signals or playing coy, as that can create unnecessary tension and hesitation.

- **Avoid the Fear of Being Too Eager**: Some men hesitate to express their feelings or intentions for fear of coming across as "too eager" or "needy." However, honesty about your intentions is powerful. A simple, "I really enjoy spending time with you and want to see where this could go" can set the right tone and communicate that you're not interested in playing games.

- **Allow for Natural Growth**: Relationships should evolve naturally, and you don't need to force or rush things. Be open to the possibility of the relationship growing at its own pace. Let the connection develop through shared experiences, meaningful conversations, and mutual discovery. This removes the pressure and lets the momentum build authentically.

3. Keep the Date and Interaction Quality High

Momentum thrives when both people feel that the connection is worth pursuing. The best way to do this is to focus on **quality interactions** that are fun, engaging, and meaningful. Relying on mind games can create superficial attraction, but creating memorable experiences will foster deeper, more lasting connection.

- **Plan Meaningful Dates**: Instead of defaulting to the usual "dinner and a movie," plan dates that create opportunities for deeper connection.

Choose activities that allow you to talk and interact naturally, such as hiking, cooking together, visiting a museum, or attending a live event. Shared experiences will give you both more to talk about, and foster a sense of **adventure and exploration**.

- **Engage Emotionally**: Momentum in a relationship comes from more than just physical attraction. Engage her emotionally by discussing deeper topics, sharing your values, and showing interest in her passions, goals, and dreams. This will deepen the connection and encourage both of you to invest more in the relationship.

- **Create Shared Experiences and Inside Jokes**: Fun, lighthearted moments and inside jokes build a unique bond between you two. Playful exchanges and moments of laughter create a natural sense of connection, which keeps the dynamic exciting without relying on manipulative tactics. These moments also foster the feeling of being part of something special, which keeps both of you invested in each other.

4. Lead with Authenticity, Not Manipulation

One of the core principles of maintaining momentum without playing games is leading with authenticity. Games thrive on **misleading behavior, manipulation**, and trying to control the outcome of interactions, but authenticity builds a much more sustainable and rewarding dynamic.

- **Be True to Yourself**: Don't try to be someone you're not to impress her or make her chase you. If you're pretending to be someone you're not, it will eventually become apparent, and it will disrupt the natural flow of your connection. Authenticity is magnetic, and by just being yourself, you'll attract someone who appreciates you for who you truly are.

- **Avoid Playing Hard to Get**: Playing hard to get is an old-school tactic that often backfires. It's not about playing "games" or creating false distance—it's about being confident enough to show your interest without overwhelming her. If you're interested, show it. If you're not, be upfront about it. **Honesty** is what leads to long-term momentum, not playing coy.

- **Lead, Don't Force**: You're not forcing anything to happen by trying to manipulate a situation. Instead, lead the interaction with strength, integrity, and respect. You want her to feel naturally drawn to you, not like she's being "led on" or strung along. Be a leader by showing confidence in who you are, maintaining strong boundaries, and treating her with respect.

5. Create a Sense of Anticipation

While it's important to keep things moving forward, it's equally important to create **space for anticipation**—something that builds excitement and keeps the momentum going without resorting to manipulative tactics. Anticipation is a natural part of attraction, and it thrives when both people are emotionally invested.

- **Don't Reveal Everything at Once**: Let the relationship unfold in layers. Instead of revealing everything about yourself immediately, allow her to discover different aspects of your personality and life over time. This creates intrigue and keeps the connection exciting. Likewise, don't feel the need to schedule every moment together. Keep her anticipating your next interaction.

- **Maintain Mystery with Grace**: You don't need to tell her every detail about your life, nor should you be an open book on the first few dates. Keeping a little mystery about your background, interests, and thoughts helps maintain intrigue. It's not about **playing games**, but allowing the relationship to develop naturally so that both of you feel that there's always more to discover about each other.

Final Thoughts: Authentic Momentum is the Key to Connection

Keeping momentum without playing games is all about **authenticity, clear communication, and mutual investment**. By focusing on building a relationship that is grounded in honesty and respect, you create the kind of dynamic that keeps both of you excited, engaged, and invested in the long term.

Avoid relying on manipulation, uncertainty, or tactics to maintain attraction—those things only build artificial connections that fade quickly.

Instead, cultivate a relationship where momentum is driven by your shared values, emotional connection, and meaningful interactions. This type of momentum is sustainable, enriching, and will naturally lead to a stronger bond and a healthier, more fulfilling relationship. When you stop playing games and start playing for real, you'll find that the connection will grow effortlessly, and both of you will be eager to see where it leads.

Building Emotional Tension and Sexual Polarity

In any romantic or intimate relationship, **emotional tension** and **sexual polarity** are the invisible forces that keep the dynamic between two people alive, exciting, and charged with energy. Without these elements, attraction can flatline, and the relationship may feel stagnant or uninspired. But when emotional tension is built correctly, and sexual polarity is in play, both partners are drawn to each other in a deeper, more powerful way—creating a natural pull that goes beyond physical attraction.

The key to creating this chemistry isn't about playing mind games or forcing anything; it's about understanding the balance between **masculine and feminine energies**, and how to leverage these dynamics to keep the relationship vibrant and dynamic.

1. Emotional Tension: The Spark That Keeps the Fire Alive

Emotional tension refers to the **underlying excitement, curiosity**, and desire that builds between two people, especially in the early stages of dating. It's that feeling of anticipation—the moments when you feel like there's something just beneath the surface, waiting to be discovered. Emotional tension doesn't have to be about constant drama or conflict, but rather the **subtle undercurrent of attraction** that keeps both of you engaged and eager for more.

- **Slow the Pace**: One of the most effective ways to build emotional tension is to **slow things down**. Rushing a connection often kills the natural build-up of attraction. Take your time to get to know each other, savor the moments, and let the curiosity grow. This doesn't mean playing games or being distant, but it does mean **holding back** just enough to leave her wanting more. Let her get a glimpse of your life, your values, and your personality, but don't give it all away at once. This gradual revealing of yourself builds a deeper emotional connection over time.

- **Create Playful Teasing and Banter**: Teasing and playful banter are incredibly effective in creating emotional tension. When done right, it keeps both of you on your toes, creates a sense of fun, and sparks an emotional connection that feels exciting and flirtatious. A little teasing can ignite that sense of mystery and anticipation without being cruel or disrespectful. Keep it light, fun, and always playful—never mean-spirited or insulting.

- **Keep Some Mystery**: Mystery is a huge part of emotional tension. If you're always fully open, always transparent, and always available, the intrigue fades away quickly. But when there's a sense of **unknown**— when she's left wondering about your thoughts, your life, or your past— you create an emotional pull that draws her in. Keep some things for later conversations, don't be an open book right away, and leave her with something to think about. A little mystery gives her the emotional space to grow interested in discovering more.

- **Escalate Gradually**: Emotional tension thrives when there is a **gradual increase in intensity**. Start by building an emotional connection that feels safe and exciting, then slowly escalate it to something more intimate. This doesn't mean rushing into physical touch or moving too fast emotionally, but it does mean progressing in a way that feels natural and stimulating. **Escalation** creates excitement, so take your time, build anticipation, and keep the energy flowing.

2. Sexual Polarity: The Dance of Masculine and Feminine Energies

Sexual polarity is the natural attraction between masculine and feminine energies. It's the **magnetic pull** that makes interactions feel intense, charged, and full of desire. To understand sexual polarity, you need to recognize the roles of **masculine energy** and **feminine energy**, and how they interact in a romantic context.

- **Masculine Energy: Strength, Direction, and Leadership**
  Masculine energy is associated with **strength, leadership**, and the ability to take decisive action. It is about providing direction, creating safety, and leading with confidence. In a dating context, this doesn't mean dominating or controlling the relationship, but instead embodying the strength of character, clarity of purpose, and the willingness to take the lead in shaping the interaction. This might look like making decisions for dates, guiding the conversation, or being confident in your intentions.

- **Feminine Energy: Openness, Nurturing, and Sensuality**
  Feminine energy, on the other hand, is rooted in **emotional fluidity**, openness, and sensuality. It is about receptivity, intuition, and being able to be emotionally expressive. Feminine energy allows for vulnerability and connection through deep emotional intimacy. This energy is what draws you in and captivates you—it's nurturing, supportive, and deeply sensual. When a woman can embrace her feminine energy, she naturally draws out your masculine energy, creating a perfect balance.

- **The Dance of Polarity**: When masculine and feminine energies interact, the **chemistry** that arises is undeniable. A woman who embraces her feminine energy creates space for the man to lead, and a man who embodies his masculine energy creates an environment where she can surrender to her femininity. This is where true **sexual polarity** happens. You both feel the dynamic tension—the push and pull that draws you closer and closer without needing to force anything. This is the essence of attraction.

- **Avoiding the Trap of Over-Comfortable Dynamics**: One of the most common pitfalls in modern relationships is the tendency to blur the lines between masculine and feminine roles. When both partners fall into comfortable, non-dynamic roles—where neither is really embracing the essence of their respective energies—the attraction can begin to fade. **Sexual polarity thrives on the tension** between masculine and feminine, and without that, the connection can become more like a friendship than a romantic bond. Ensure that both energies are respected and celebrated in your dynamic, as this is what keeps the sexual attraction strong.

3. The Role of Tension in Creating Desire

Desire is sparked when both people feel a **build-up of energy**—an intensity that keeps them thinking about each other even after they've parted ways. Building emotional tension and sexual polarity isn't about playing hard to get or creating distance for the sake of control; it's about allowing attraction to build naturally by creating opportunities for **desire** to grow.

- **Physical Touch to Build Intensity**: Physical touch is a powerful way to create emotional tension and intensify sexual polarity. Light touches, such as a hand on her back, brushing her arm, or a lingering touch on her shoulder, build an intimate atmosphere without rushing into full physical intimacy. These subtle gestures create a sense of **closeness** and build anticipation. When the touch is slow and deliberate, it amplifies the tension, making the moments of deeper connection feel more profound.

- **Seduction Is About More Than Sex**: Seduction isn't just about the physical act; it's about creating an **emotional connection** that leads to desire. The most powerful seduction is a combination of emotional vulnerability and confidence. When you create a space where both of you feel free to express your desires, while maintaining the right balance of masculine strength and feminine receptivity, the sexual tension will build organically.

- **The Subtle Art of Teasing and Flirting**: Teasing and flirting are both essential tools for maintaining emotional tension and sexual polarity. They should always be playful and light-hearted, never crossing into negativity or making the other person feel uncomfortable. When done correctly, flirting creates an **intangible connection** that leaves both of you eager to explore more. This teasing shouldn't be overdone, but used strategically to **maintain the tension** between you.

4. Balancing Passion with Respect

While sexual tension and emotional polarity are crucial to creating attraction, they should always be balanced with **respect and emotional safety**. Too much tension without enough respect can turn a relationship into a game of power struggles, while too much ease without tension can leave the connection feeling flat. The best relationships maintain a **dynamic balance** between **passion** and **safety**—creating an atmosphere where desire can flourish, but both people feel emotionally seen, heard, and respected.

- **Respect Boundaries**: The polarity between masculine and feminine energy should always exist within the confines of **respectful interaction**. Sexual tension is exciting, but only when both people feel emotionally safe and respected in the process. Pay attention to her comfort level, and make sure that both of you are progressing at a pace that feels right for the relationship.

- **Honor the Emotional Connection**: Emotional connection is the bedrock upon which sexual attraction thrives. Never sacrifice the emotional bond for the sake of physical intensity. True attraction grows out of both **emotional depth** and sexual chemistry. When both are present, the relationship becomes more fulfilling and exciting, and the intensity never fades.

Final Thoughts: Cultivating Sustainable Attraction

Emotional tension and sexual polarity are the forces that keep attraction alive, but they must be cultivated with care and intention. By building emotional tension gradually, embracing the natural dance between masculine and feminine energies, and respecting each other's boundaries, you create an environment where the attraction can not only grow but thrive over time.

Remember: the goal is not to create **artificial tension** or manipulate each other, but to understand the natural dynamics of attraction and work with them.

When you build this tension in a respectful, genuine way, the result is a powerful, magnetic connection that will carry the relationship forward with excitement, desire, and depth.

9

Long-Term Connection – Keeping Her (Without Losing Yourself)

How to Maintain Attraction Over Time

In the early stages of a relationship, attraction often comes easily. The excitement, the newness, the rush of learning about each other—everything feels like a natural spark. However, as time passes, it can be easy for that initial intensity to fade. The challenge then becomes how to **maintain attraction** over the long term. How do you keep the connection vibrant, passionate, and alive, without falling into the trap of complacency or losing sight of who you are?

The key to maintaining attraction isn't about constant effort, games, or keeping up appearances. It's about creating an environment where **authenticity, growth, and mutual respect** can thrive. Attraction is something that needs to be nurtured, not forced, and it must be rooted in deep emotional and physical connection. Here's how to do it:

1. Stay True to Yourself – Be the Man She Fell For

One of the biggest mistakes men make in long-term relationships is compromising who they are in order to **please their partner** or avoid conflict. Over time, this can lead to resentment and a loss of attraction. **The key to maintaining attraction is being the man she fell for**—staying aligned with your core values, passions, and purpose.

- **Never Lose Sight of Your Own Identity**: As a relationship deepens, it's easy to start putting the other person's needs first, but you must remember to stay rooted in who you are. Continue pursuing your passions, keeping up with your personal goals, and staying committed to

165

your own growth. This self-respect and independence create the foundation for her to remain attracted to you. When you feel **fulfilled and confident in your own life**, that energy is magnetic and keeps the attraction alive.

- **Don't Fall into Routine Complacency**: While routines can provide stability, they can also lead to boredom if you let them dictate your relationship. **Avoid getting stuck in the "same old"** patterns. Keep surprising her with spontaneous gestures, new activities, and new sides of yourself. You want her to feel like there is always something fresh and exciting about you, even if it's been years since you first met.

2. Continue to Build Emotional Intimacy

Emotional intimacy is the foundation of **long-term attraction**. The longer you're together, the deeper your emotional bond should grow. If you stop connecting emotionally, physical attraction will begin to dwindle as well. Building emotional intimacy means creating a space where both of you can be vulnerable, honest, and deeply connected.

- **Engage in Deep Conversations**: As time goes on, you may find yourselves having the same conversations over and over again. Instead, challenge yourselves to dig deeper. Share your dreams, fears, and evolving thoughts about life, and encourage her to do the same. When you connect emotionally, it's easier to stay connected physically. Emotional intimacy brings you closer, making your bond even stronger.

- **Make Her Feel Heard and Valued**: Feeling truly heard and understood is one of the most powerful forms of intimacy. Listen actively to her, show empathy, and validate her feelings. When she feels emotionally safe with you, it makes her more likely to stay invested in the relationship. Show that you value her thoughts, ideas, and emotions, and she will continue to feel drawn to you.

- **Handle Conflict with Emotional Maturity**: In any long-term relationship, there will be disagreements. How you handle these moments is critical to maintaining attraction. **Avoid being defensive** or aggressive during arguments. Instead, approach conflicts with a mindset of growth and understanding. When both partners can handle difficult conversations with maturity, it strengthens the relationship and enhances the emotional connection.

3. Keep Physical Intimacy Exciting

Sexual attraction tends to shift over time. What was once spontaneous and passionate can become routine or even feel absent if not nurtured. **Physical intimacy** is a cornerstone of attraction, and keeping that spark alive requires **intentional effort**. It's not about constant novelty or constantly trying to impress, but rather about maintaining connection, curiosity, and the willingness to invest in each other.

- **Don't Let Sex Become a Chore**: Many couples fall into a pattern where intimacy becomes predictable, and they stop putting effort into keeping it exciting. **Be intentional about making intimacy a priority.** Experiment with new ways of connecting physically, whether it's through a romantic date night, exploring different ways to connect in bed, or simply taking the time to focus on each other's pleasure. Emotional and physical intimacy should be mutually satisfying, with both partners showing care and attention to the other's needs.

- **Make Time for Physical Connection Beyond Sex**: Physical attraction isn't just about sex—it's about **touch** and affection in the small moments, too. Hold hands, cuddle, kiss without the expectation of it leading to sex. Physical connection should be ongoing and non-sexual at times, so it doesn't feel like something you only do when the goal is sex. **Make her feel desired and cherished** by simply showing affection in ways that are consistent with your love language.

- **Stay Physically Attractive**: While attraction isn't just about looks, **staying physically fit and healthy** does play a role in maintaining attraction. Make sure you're taking care of your body, whether that's through exercise, eating well, or grooming. When you prioritize your own health and fitness, it not only makes you feel good but also makes you more attractive to your partner.

4. Continue to Lead in the Relationship

One of the qualities that many women find attractive in a long-term partner is a sense of **strong leadership**. Not in the sense of being controlling, but in the sense of being decisive, clear in your actions, and maintaining a strong sense of purpose.

- **Stay a Leader in Your Own Life**: A strong, attractive man is one who leads with confidence—not just in the relationship, but in his own life. Whether it's your career, your hobbies, or your vision for the future, continue to lead your life with purpose and clarity. **Women are attracted to men who have direction**, and who can make decisions and take action with certainty. Your leadership extends beyond guiding the relationship—it's about how you show up in every area of your life.

- **Be the Protector and Provider**: This doesn't mean just financially (although that can be part of it). **Being a protector** also means being emotionally strong, offering a sense of stability and security, and being there for her in ways that let her know you're committed to the relationship. Show her that you are someone she can rely on, both emotionally and practically.

- **Don't Let the Relationship Stall**: A relationship without leadership can quickly feel stagnant. Keep making decisions, whether it's planning trips, choosing activities, or taking the next step in your connection. **Keep moving forward together** with intentionality. The more you lead in a way that is collaborative and supportive, the more she will stay connected to you.

5. Keep the Fun and Adventure Alive

One of the easiest ways to let a relationship go stale is to stop having fun together. Over time, the mundane aspects of life can overshadow the excitement and adventure that initially brought you together. Keeping the relationship fun doesn't mean constantly trying to outdo yourself with grand gestures, but it does mean staying open to new experiences and **embracing spontaneity**.

- **Plan New Adventures**: Surprise her with a fun date, a weekend getaway, or a new activity that pushes both of you out of your comfort zones. Trying new things together not only keeps things fresh but also deepens your bond as you share new experiences.

- **Laugh Together**: Humor is an often overlooked, yet incredibly powerful tool in keeping attraction alive. Laughter is bonding—it creates a sense of lightness and joy that makes spending time together enjoyable. Keep the playful side of your relationship alive, and never underestimate the power of shared laughter to keep the connection strong.

- **Create New Memories**: As you move forward together, always strive to create new memories. They don't have to be big moments. It could be something as simple as taking a walk at night, trying a new recipe together, or watching a movie you've both been wanting to see. These little moments of shared joy build emotional intimacy and connection, and give both of you something to look back on fondly.

Final Thoughts: Love and Attraction Are Ongoing Investments

Attraction in a long-term relationship is not something that can be taken for granted. It's not static. Just because you've found someone you love doesn't mean you stop working on the connection. **Maintaining attraction over time requires ongoing effort**, but it's the kind of effort that pays off with a relationship that remains dynamic, passionate, and fulfilling.

By staying true to yourself, deepening emotional intimacy, nurturing physical connection, leading with purpose, and keeping the fun and adventure alive, you create a relationship that is both meaningful and exciting. You're not just keeping her attracted to you—you're building a bond that can stand the test of time, a connection that continues to grow, evolve, and thrive.

Balancing Vulnerability and Strength

In any successful, long-term relationship, the balance between **vulnerability** and **strength** is essential. These two qualities are not opposites but complementary forces that, when harmonized, create a powerful dynamic of trust, respect, and attraction. Many men struggle with the idea of vulnerability, fearing that it will make them seem weak or less attractive. But the truth is, **embracing vulnerability** alongside maintaining strength is one of the most effective ways to deepen your connection with a woman and foster a relationship that is both emotionally rich and grounded in respect.

1. Understanding Vulnerability: Strength in Openness

Vulnerability is often misunderstood as weakness, but it is anything but. Vulnerability is the **courage to be open**, to show parts of yourself that are typically hidden, and to allow another person to see you in your raw, unguarded state. It's not about oversharing or exposing yourself to emotional harm; it's about having the **confidence** to share your true feelings, fears, desires, and insecurities in a way that fosters deeper intimacy.

- **Vulnerability Builds Trust**: When you allow yourself to be vulnerable, you show a woman that you trust her enough to open up. This **shared emotional honesty** creates a deep sense of connection, as it signals that you value her presence in your life and are willing to be authentic. It tells her that you are comfortable with who you are, imperfections and all— and this authenticity is magnetic.

- **Vulnerability Creates Emotional Depth**: Relationships without emotional depth can feel shallow. **Vulnerability invites emotional intimacy** by creating a space where both partners can express their true selves without judgment. Sharing personal thoughts, fears, or dreams allows the relationship to mature beyond superficial interactions and evolve into something much more meaningful.

- **Expressing Your Needs**: Being vulnerable also means being able to express your needs—whether they are emotional, physical, or psychological. It's easy to slip into the trap of expecting someone to intuitively know what you need, but this only creates frustration and miscommunication. **Articulate your desires** and concerns clearly and respectfully, which not only strengthens your emotional bond but also teaches her how to best support you.

2. The Role of Strength: Confidence and Stability

While vulnerability is about showing your authentic self, strength is about embodying **confidence, resilience**, and the ability to lead in your life and relationship. Strength isn't about being infallible or always in control, but about **having inner certainty and emotional stability**, especially during challenging times.

- **Strength is Emotional Control**: The true mark of strength is **emotional regulation**. It's being able to stay grounded even when life throws challenges your way. When you stay composed and calm, even in the face of adversity, you provide a sense of **security and stability** for your partner. This is incredibly attractive and reassuring, as it signals that you are someone who can handle stress and uncertainty without being overwhelmed by them.

- **Strength is Leadership and Direction**: Being strong means leading with clarity and confidence in your decisions, whether they are about your career, the direction of the relationship, or the day-to-day logistics of your life together. A woman wants a partner who has a **clear vision** for where he's headed and the ability to take decisive action. This type of strength creates a sense of security and makes the relationship feel anchored and purposeful.

- **Strength is Boundaries and Self-Respect**: Strength also comes from having **healthy boundaries** and a strong sense of self-respect. You don't tolerate disrespect or settle for less than what you deserve. You communicate clearly when something isn't working for you, and you are **unapologetically yourself**, no matter the situation. When you embody self-respect and self-assurance, it's easier to maintain a strong and balanced relationship.

3. The Power of Balance: Integrating Vulnerability and Strength

When vulnerability and strength are integrated into your personality and actions, they form a dynamic, attractive balance. The ideal balance is not about choosing one over the other but about knowing when to be strong and when to show vulnerability. Too much vulnerability without strength can lead to emotional exhaustion or being perceived as overly dependent, while too much strength without vulnerability can create emotional distance or make the relationship feel cold and unfeeling.

- **Strength Enables Vulnerability**: Paradoxically, it is often **strength that makes vulnerability possible**. The more confident and emotionally grounded you are, the more willing you will be to open up. You're not afraid of being judged or rejected because you trust your own sense of self-worth. Strength gives you the courage to take the emotional risk of being vulnerable.

- **Vulnerability Enhances Strength**: Conversely, vulnerability actually enhances strength by making you more **human** and accessible. It allows your partner to see that you're not invincible, and that you too experience struggles and doubts. This authenticity creates a deeper connection, as she can empathize with your challenges. It also invites her to be vulnerable with you in return, deepening the emotional intimacy of the relationship.

- **Timing and Context Matter**: The art of balancing these qualities lies in knowing when to show vulnerability and when to embody strength. For example, **during tough times** or when you face an emotional hurdle, it's okay to express your fears, frustrations, or uncertainties. It's an opportunity to lean on your partner and show that you trust her. However, in moments of decision-making, stress, or external challenges, you should demonstrate strength by **staying composed, making decisions, and taking charge** where necessary.

4. The Impact on Your Relationship

- **Creating a Deeper Connection**: A relationship where both partners can be vulnerable without feeling exposed, and strong without being cold, creates a **profound emotional bond**. Vulnerability allows you to see each other's humanity, while strength provides a foundation of safety and support. The dynamic becomes one of mutual respect and understanding, where both partners feel secure in their emotional expression.

- **Nurturing Long-Term Attraction**: Long-term attraction depends not only on physical chemistry but also on emotional connection. A relationship based on vulnerability and strength has staying power. By embracing both aspects, you create a dynamic that allows for **emotional intimacy** to evolve over time without falling into complacency or stagnation.

- **Respecting Each Other's Needs**: The key to long-term success is **mutual respect**. When you balance vulnerability and strength, you make space for your partner to express her own needs and desires without fear of judgment. This reciprocal openness strengthens the foundation of your relationship, as both partners feel valued for their authentic selves.

Final Thoughts: Vulnerability and Strength are the Cornerstones of Growth

To maintain a thriving relationship, **vulnerability and strength must coexist**. The ideal partner is one who can be open and emotionally honest, while also standing firm in their values, goals, and the ability to lead. Embracing both qualities allows you to build a deep, lasting connection that is rooted in mutual respect, emotional depth, and true intimacy.

When you understand how to navigate the delicate balance between vulnerability and strength, you unlock a level of connection that fosters true intimacy and keeps the relationship evolving in an authentic, sustainable way. In the end, this balance is what ensures the attraction and emotional bond remain strong over time.

Leadership in Relationships: Setting the Tone

Leadership in relationships isn't about being controlling or domineering; it's about creating an environment where both partners can thrive, feel supported, and grow together. As a man, stepping into a **leadership role** in your relationship means you are actively shaping the emotional climate, guiding the connection, and setting the tone for how you both interact and navigate life's challenges. It's about **embodying responsibility**, **showing emotional intelligence**, and **taking initiative** in a way that fosters mutual respect, trust, and deeper intimacy.

While many people think of leadership in a relationship as being about **making decisions** or **taking charge** at every turn, the true essence of leadership lies in your ability to be present, aware, and purposeful. The way you show up for your partner sets the standard for how the relationship will unfold. Here's how you can set the right tone and become the kind of leader that attracts respect, loyalty, and love:

1. Lead with Purpose and Vision

In any successful relationship, direction and vision are crucial. **Being the leader means having a clear sense of purpose** not only for your own life but for the relationship as a whole. Where are you both headed together? What are the values that guide your relationship? What do you both want to create in your lives together?

- **Clarify Your Values**: Leadership begins with clarity of vision. Know what is important to you, what you stand for, and what you want in the relationship. When you have a clear direction and purpose, it becomes easier to make decisions and create an atmosphere of mutual understanding. Lead by example by aligning your actions with the values you want to see in the relationship, whether it's **honesty, trust, growth**, or **adventure**.

- **Create a Shared Vision**: The role of a leader is not just to dictate but to **inspire** and unite. Discuss the direction you want the relationship to take and establish goals together. Do you want to travel more? Build financial stability? Deepen your emotional connection? Whatever it is, a good leader ensures that both people in the relationship have a stake in the future and are moving toward it in harmony.

- **Be the Guiding Hand, Not the Dictator**: Leadership in relationships isn't about making all the decisions or controlling every situation. It's about **creating an atmosphere where both partners feel seen and heard**. When you lead with purpose, your actions speak louder than your words, creating a shared vision that motivates both of you to grow together.

2. Emotional Leadership: Create a Safe Space for Emotional Expression

One of the most powerful aspects of leadership in relationships is emotional intelligence. Being a leader in the emotional sphere of the relationship means guiding your partner through **ups and downs** with empathy, compassion, and emotional control.

- **Stay Grounded in Difficult Situations**: As a leader, you set the emotional tone of the relationship. If you allow yourself to be **controlled by negative emotions**, it can throw off the balance and create tension. However, if you remain calm, composed, and grounded during difficult moments, you show your partner that you are capable of navigating life's challenges with maturity and stability.

- **Encourage Emotional Vulnerability**: Leadership in relationships also means being open about your own emotions, creating space for your partner to express herself honestly and without fear of judgment. By showing vulnerability and openness, you invite her to do the same. This reciprocal emotional sharing creates deeper intimacy and trust, which are essential for a strong connection.

- **Manage Conflict with Grace**: In relationships, conflict is inevitable, but how you handle it determines the quality of the connection. **A strong leader in the relationship approaches conflict** with patience, understanding, and a mindset of resolution rather than winning. You listen actively, acknowledge your partner's feelings, and work collaboratively toward solutions. By doing so, you build emotional trust and set a positive example for resolving disagreements respectfully.

3. Lead by Example: Actions Speak Louder Than Words

Leadership in relationships is rooted in action. Your partner looks to you for **consistency** and **integrity**—the way you behave, show up, and handle life's challenges will set the tone for how the relationship unfolds.

- **Demonstrate Strength and Stability**: A great leader doesn't just talk about values—he lives them. Whether it's how you handle stress, pursue your personal goals, or support your partner, your actions are a reflection of your **character**. If you value hard work and resilience, demonstrate it in your own life. If you value kindness and compassion, show it consistently in your interactions. Your partner will follow your lead, and together, you'll create a solid foundation built on mutual respect.

- **Be Reliable and Dependable**: Leadership isn't about always having the answers—it's about being someone your partner can rely on. Be consistent in your actions and trustworthy in your words. When you make commitments, follow through. When you offer support, be there. Your reliability strengthens the bond and reassures your partner that they can count on you, no matter the circumstances.

- **Demonstrate Self-Improvement and Growth**: Great leaders are never stagnant; they are always evolving, learning, and striving for better. To lead in a relationship, you need to **model self-growth and improvement**. Whether it's personal development, pursuing new skills, or improving your communication, show your partner that you are committed to **growing both individually and as a couple**. This will inspire her to do the same, which leads to a dynamic, evolving relationship.

4. Lead with Confidence and Decisiveness

A strong leader in a relationship is not afraid to make decisions, take responsibility, and move forward with confidence. While a partnership requires collaboration and compromise, there are moments when **decisiveness** is essential.

- **Take Initiative**: Leading a relationship means taking initiative when it's necessary. Whether it's planning dates, handling logistical issues, or making important decisions, **don't wait for your partner to always take the reins**. Take the lead, and do so with confidence. This shows that you are engaged, capable, and invested in the well-being of the relationship.

- **Be Assertive, Not Aggressive**: Leadership involves knowing when to step up and make decisions, but also respecting your partner's input. **Assertiveness** is the ability to express your thoughts, needs, and desires confidently, while also remaining open to discussion. Assertiveness allows you to maintain your leadership role without becoming domineering or dismissive of your partner's voice.

- **Take Responsibility for Mistakes**: Being a leader also means **owning up to your mistakes**. When things don't go as planned, take responsibility rather than deflecting blame. This creates an environment of mutual respect and accountability, where both partners feel comfortable learning and growing from their experiences.

5. Be a Source of Inspiration and Motivation

Leadership in relationships also involves being an **inspiration** to your partner. Your actions and attitude can serve as a motivating force that encourages your partner to pursue her own goals and dreams.

- **Support Her Goals**: A great leader doesn't just focus on his own ambitions—he supports his partner in her endeavors as well. Encourage her to **pursue her passions**, and be her biggest cheerleader. Show her that you believe in her and that her dreams are just as important as your own. When both partners inspire each other, the relationship becomes a powerful force for growth.

- **Cultivate Positivity**: As a leader, your mindset can be contagious. If you consistently approach life with a positive attitude, a sense of humor, and an unwavering belief in the potential of the relationship, you inspire your partner to adopt a similar outlook. Your **energy and optimism** can help your partner navigate difficult times and encourage both of you to keep moving forward together.

- **Lead in the Everyday Moments**: Leadership isn't just about the big decisions—it's about the little moments, too. Whether it's how you treat each other day-to-day, how you show appreciation, or how you support each other in everyday tasks, your leadership **sets the tone for the**

relationship's overall vibe. Lead with kindness, respect, and purpose, and your relationship will flourish.

Final Thoughts: Leadership Creates a Thriving Relationship

Being a leader in your relationship doesn't mean you have to dominate or control—it means that you take responsibility for your actions, set a strong example, and guide the relationship with integrity, confidence, and compassion. By leading with purpose, emotional intelligence, decisiveness, and mutual respect, you create an environment where both you and your partner can grow and thrive.

When you set the tone through strong, conscious leadership, you inspire your partner to do the same, creating a dynamic, thriving relationship built on trust, respect, and shared goals. This leadership brings out the best in both partners and makes the connection not just a partnership but a **journey of mutual growth and fulfilment**.

Avoiding Co-Dependency and Staying on Mission

In the pursuit of a fulfilling and successful relationship, one of the most critical aspects to understand is the fine line between **interdependence** and **co-dependency**. Co-dependency is a destructive dynamic where two people rely on each other to meet emotional needs in unhealthy, often unbalanced ways. It can strip both individuals of their sense of self and prevent growth, both personally and as a couple. On the other hand, **interdependence** is the foundation of a strong relationship—where both individuals retain their identity and independence while also supporting one another in meaningful, mutually beneficial ways.

The challenge is knowing how to avoid slipping into **co-dependency** and instead focus on maintaining your **personal mission**, goals, and independence, all while nurturing a thriving partnership. Here's how you can avoid co-dependency and stay on mission, both in your relationship and in your life:

1. Prioritize Your Individual Growth

A strong, healthy relationship is one where both partners are committed to **personal development** and **growth**. If you are neglecting your own ambitions, passions, and goals to focus entirely on the relationship, you risk becoming emotionally entangled and overly reliant on your partner for validation and fulfilment. This is where co-dependency can creep in.

- **Stay Focused on Your Mission**: Keep your personal goals at the forefront of your life. Whether it's building your career, pursuing hobbies, staying fit, or growing spiritually, **you must remain dedicated to your own personal development**. This ensures that you don't lose sight of your identity in the relationship and keeps you emotionally balanced. Your partner should complement your life, not consume it.

- **Invest in Your Emotional Health**: Practice **emotional self-care**— take the time to process your feelings, work through past baggage, and engage in activities that help you maintain emotional well-being. This prevents you from relying on your partner to "fix" your emotional problems, which can be a hallmark of co-dependency.

- **Support Her Growth, But Don't Enable**: Just as you focus on your own growth, support your partner's growth as well. A thriving relationship involves **two independent individuals** who support and encourage each other's missions and personal goals. Avoid the trap of enabling each other's bad habits or emotional dependencies, and instead, encourage each other to be your best selves.

2. Set Boundaries to Protect Your Independence

Boundaries are essential to preventing co-dependency. Without healthy boundaries, it's easy to lose yourself in the relationship, surrender your emotional autonomy, and become too enmeshed with your partner. This is where codependent patterns often emerge—when one partner starts to **overgive**, sacrificing their needs for the other, while the other becomes overly reliant on them.

- **Know Your Limits**: Understand your **emotional, mental, and physical limits** and communicate them clearly with your partner.

Whether it's about how much time you need for yourself, how much emotional energy you can give, or what you're willing to tolerate, setting clear boundaries ensures that your needs are met without compromising your sense of self.

- **Create Space for Yourself**: Make sure you have time and space to recharge. Whether it's spending time alone, pursuing hobbies, or catching up with friends, **taking time for yourself** isn't selfish—it's essential for maintaining a healthy sense of independence. A partner who respects your need for space is someone who understands the importance of interdependence.

- **Communicate Effectively**: If you ever feel like your boundaries are being pushed, address the issue early. Don't let resentment build up or allow yourself to be dragged into unhealthy dynamics. Speak honestly and assertively about your needs and ask for the space or respect you need to feel balanced.

3. Cultivate Emotional Self-Sufficiency

Co-dependency often arises when one person starts to rely heavily on their partner for **emotional regulation**—looking to them for constant validation, support, or reassurance. This creates an unhealthy cycle where both partners become emotionally drained, and one or both may begin to feel overwhelmed or trapped.

- **Know How to Self-Regulate**: **Emotional self-sufficiency** is a crucial skill. Learn how to process and manage your emotions without relying on your partner for constant emotional support. Practice healthy coping strategies like mindfulness, journaling, exercising, or meditating. When you can regulate your emotions on your own, you reduce the emotional burden on your partner and prevent codependent patterns from developing.

- **Validate Yourself**: You should be your **own source of validation**. While it's natural and healthy to seek appreciation and affection from your partner, you shouldn't base your self-worth solely on their approval. Practice affirmations, focus on your personal accomplishments, and **build confidence** through self-reliance. When you maintain a strong sense of self-worth, you are less likely to fall into the trap of seeking constant reassurance from your partner.

4. Maintain a Sense of Purpose Outside of the Relationship

One of the best ways to avoid co-dependency is to make sure you have a **purpose** that extends beyond the relationship. While a partnership can be deeply fulfilling, it should never be the **sole source of your happiness or fulfilment**. If you lose sight of your personal goals or interests and allow the relationship to become the center of your world, co-dependency can easily set in.

- **Pursue Meaningful Activities**: Whether it's advancing in your career, engaging in creative pursuits, or building a community, make sure that your life has purpose beyond your relationship. This helps you stay grounded in who you are as an individual, rather than defining yourself solely through your partner.

- **Keep Expanding Your Horizons**: The best relationships involve two people who continue to grow, explore, and challenge themselves. Don't let the relationship become a **stagnant space** where personal growth is sidelined. Continue exploring new ideas, setting goals, and taking action to fulfill your personal mission. This ensures that you both stay vibrant and engaged, which ultimately strengthens the bond you share.

5. Stay Empowered in the Relationship Dynamic

A healthy relationship dynamic is one where both partners feel empowered, capable, and **equal** in their contributions. In a co-dependent relationship, one partner may unconsciously take on the role of the "caretaker" or the "fixer," which can result in an **imbalance of power**. The key is to remain **empowered** within the relationship by maintaining a sense of self-respect, independence, and mutual support.

- **Lead by Example**: Empowerment comes from being proactive, assertive, and taking responsibility for your own actions. Show up in the relationship as someone who is **driven, responsible,** and **confident** in your ability to handle challenges. When you empower yourself, you naturally inspire your partner to do the same.

- **Ensure Mutual Respect**: Healthy relationships are built on a foundation of mutual respect, not one person constantly giving and the other constantly taking. **Respect your partner's needs** and goals while expecting the same in return. This balance ensures that you both remain independent and strong in the relationship.

Final Thoughts: Stay on Mission and Protect Your Independence

To avoid co-dependency, it's crucial to focus on **individual growth, maintaining boundaries**, and **ensuring emotional self-sufficiency**. A healthy relationship is one where both partners maintain their individual sense of self while supporting each other in meaningful ways.

By staying **mission-driven**, continuously pursuing your goals, and setting clear boundaries, you ensure that your relationship will be **based on mutual respect and interdependence**, not unhealthy reliance. Remember, a relationship should be a place where both partners grow together—not a place where they lose themselves in each other.

When you remain grounded in your own purpose and empowered in the relationship, you'll not only avoid co-dependency but also create a relationship that is strong, fulfilling, and sustainable for the long term.

Growth as a Couple vs. Growth as a Man

When you enter into a committed relationship, it's easy to think of growth as a shared journey—one where both you and your partner evolve together. And while this is certainly true, it's important to remember that growth as a man and growth as a couple are two distinct but complementary aspects of your personal and relational development. Balancing both requires self-awareness, intentionality, and a clear understanding of how each growth path intersects and enhances the other.

In this section, we'll explore the difference between growth as a man—your personal development, individual goals, and self-discovery—and growth as a couple, which involves building a thriving, dynamic relationship that encourages both partners to reach their highest potential together.

1. Growth as a Man: Building a Strong Foundation for Yourself

Growth as a man is about becoming the best version of yourself, independently from your partner. This journey is rooted in your personal values, goals, ambitions, and emotional maturity. It involves taking ownership of your life and evolving into a confident, capable, and resilient individual who brings value to the relationship—not as a means of validation, but because you've cultivated your worth and sense of purpose on your own.

Building Personal Strength

The growth of a man starts with self-awareness. This means taking a hard look at your strengths, weaknesses, past experiences, and the areas in your life that need improvement. Whether it's your physical health, emotional intelligence, career ambitions, or personal passions, your growth is a continuous, lifelong journey that requires discipline, self-reflection, and action.

For example, if you're focused on building your physical health, your growth as a man will come from committing to a consistent workout regimen, learning about nutrition, and creating a lifestyle that enhances your strength and vitality. Similarly, emotional growth might involve addressing past traumas, developing your communication skills, or cultivating a healthy relationship with your emotions.

Independence and Self-Sufficiency

Growth as a man also means maintaining your independence. This doesn't mean that you disregard your partner or don't invest in the relationship, but rather that you maintain a strong sense of self and pursue your own goals, passions, and ambitions. When you are emotionally self-sufficient, you bring stability, confidence, and a sense of direction to the relationship, which empowers both you and your partner to thrive.

By focusing on growth as a man, you develop the strength and clarity needed to lead your own life, whether that's through career development, cultivating meaningful friendships, or deepening your understanding of who you are. This sense of personal fulfilment and purpose is essential to bring into any relationship, ensuring you don't lose yourself or sacrifice your personal goals for the sake of the relationship.

2. Growth as a Couple: Evolving Together Through Shared Vision

Growth as a couple, on the other hand, is the process of building a deep, meaningful relationship that allows both partners to flourish as individuals while fostering a strong sense of togetherness. It's about creating a shared vision, aligning your values, and continually nurturing your connection to ensure that you both grow in harmony.

Developing Mutual Respect and Trust

For growth as a couple to occur, both partners must be committed to creating a relationship grounded in mutual respect, trust, and understanding. Each partner must actively listen to the other's needs, be open to compromise, and continuously work together toward common goals. As you deepen your connection, you'll learn how to navigate conflict, build empathy, and create an environment where both of you feel valued and heard.

This shared journey of growth also requires emotional intimacy—being able to open up to one another, share vulnerabilities, and support each other through life's challenges. When you both commit to evolving emotionally together, you create a bond that's not only built on love but also mutual understanding and shared experiences.

Shared Goals and Vision

Growth as a couple also involves aligning your visions for the future. Whether it's building a family, pursuing financial goals, or working together on a passion project, having a shared sense of purpose will help you stay united, even when external challenges arise. Regularly discussing your dreams, values, and life goals ensures that you both remain on the same path and can support each other's aspirations.

For example, if you and your partner both value personal growth but have different approaches to how you want to pursue it, you can find ways to support each other's individual goals while continuing to nurture the relationship. The key is ensuring that your growth paths do not diverge in ways that undermine the relationship's foundation. Instead, encourage one another's growth, and use it as a springboard for mutual support and evolution.

3. How Personal Growth Enhances Couple Growth

While growth as a man is essential to becoming a strong, capable partner, it's also crucial for enhancing the relationship itself. When you focus on developing yourself, you bring clarity, emotional stability, and strength to the relationship, which encourages your partner to do the same. Personal growth also helps you navigate challenges with resilience, and it strengthens your ability to communicate openly, handle conflict constructively, and maintain a healthy emotional connection.

The more self-aware and emotionally mature you become as an individual, the more you have to offer to your relationship. As you pursue your own personal goals, you show your partner that growth is a lifelong journey. This not only inspires them to continue evolving as well but also fosters a growth mindset within the relationship.

4. How Couple Growth Enhances Personal Growth

On the flip side, growth as a couple can directly impact your personal growth. A relationship can be a powerful catalyst for self-improvement when both partners are aligned and committed to growing together. The support, love, and accountability that come from a deep partnership can push both individuals to step outside their comfort zones, take risks, and pursue goals they might not have tackled on their own.

As a couple, you will often encounter challenges that force you to evolve—whether it's navigating difficult situations, learning how to compromise, or simply growing into new versions of yourselves. By facing these challenges together, you build strength, resilience, and adaptive skills that will help you in every aspect of your life, both individually and within the relationship.

5. Balancing the Two Forms of Growth

The key to thriving in both areas—personal growth as a man and growth as a couple—is balance. While it's essential that you invest in your individual growth, you also need to remain committed to the growth of the relationship. Both growth paths are symbiotic, and when one area is neglected, the other suffers.

To balance these two types of growth, consider the following strategies:

- Communicate openly with your partner about your personal goals and how they fit into the larger picture of the relationship. This helps create alignment between your individual and shared goals.

- Create space for both types of growth. Dedicate time to your personal development through hobbies, fitness, or self-reflection, while also setting aside time for quality time, communication, and collaboration as a couple.

- Support each other's growth journeys. Celebrate each other's wins, encourage each other through challenges, and always show up for one another's personal goals.

Final Thoughts: Growth as a Man and Growth as a Couple Are Interdependent

Ultimately, growth as a man and growth as a couple aren't opposing forces—they are interdependent. The more you invest in yourself and become the best version of who you are, the more you have to offer to the relationship. And the stronger the relationship becomes, the more support and motivation you'll find to keep evolving as an individual.

By balancing these two types of growth—personal and relational—you create a life that's not only fulfilling for both you and your partner but one that allows both of you to continue growing together, building a future based on mutual respect, shared dreams, and unwavering support.

Conclusion – You are the Prize

Reflecting on the Journey from Weakness to Strength

As we come to the end of this journey, it's important to pause and reflect on how far you've come—the transformation from weakness to strength. The path you've taken is not just about **learning strategies** or applying techniques, but about **embracing your personal evolution**. In this final section, let's take a moment to celebrate your progress and recognize the deep internal shifts that have occurred as you've walked through this process of growth.

The Power of Awareness

The first step in this journey often begins with awareness—the realization that where you are isn't where you want to be. This might have shown up in the form of frustration with past dating experiences, dissatisfaction with how you were showing up in your life, or a feeling of being stuck or powerless. The moment you acknowledge that change is necessary, you've already taken the first powerful step.

At the beginning, you may have felt like you were operating from a place of weakness—whether it was due to self-doubt, lack of direction, low confidence, or unhealthy patterns that sabotaged your relationships. But this awareness is the seed of your strength. It's the moment you chose to **look inward**, face the uncomfortable truths about yourself, and commit to building a better, more empowered version of who you are.

Building Strength through Discipline

As you began to apply the principles of discipline, consistency, and self-respect, you started to notice real change. Discipline became your greatest ally, not as a source of rigid control, but as the fuel that powered your transformation. Through every setback, challenge, and difficult moment, you learned that strength isn't built in moments of ease but through **embracing discomfort** and pushing yourself beyond your limits. Each time you made a choice to stay focused on your growth instead of falling back into old habits, you were **reinforcing your mental and emotional resilience**.

In this process, the concept of **strength** shifted. Strength was no longer about appearing tough or invulnerable—it became a reflection of your ability to **persevere through adversity**, to **learn from failure**, and to **maintain your values** even in the face of temptation or difficulty. You built emotional control, learned to assert your boundaries, and embraced your masculinity as something dynamic and authentic, not something you had to prove.

From Dependency to Independence

One of the most powerful aspects of this transformation was the shift from **dependence** to **independence**—not just in your relationships, but in how you view yourself. The dependency on validation from external sources—whether it be from others' opinions, societal expectations, or even your partner—began to dissolve. In its place, you developed a solid sense of **self-worth** that wasn't reliant on others' approval.

Through developing quiet confidence, practicing emotional control, and learning to lead with authenticity, you built a **rock-solid foundation** that could weather the storms of life. You no longer felt the need to chase or cling to anyone or anything for fulfilment. Instead, you recognized that **you are the prize**, and the people in your life should add value to your already rich existence, not define it.

Embracing Masculine Leadership

As your personal development deepened, so too did your understanding of masculine leadership—both in your life and in your relationships. The more you focused on becoming **purpose-driven, disciplined**, and **emotionally intelligent**, the more you attracted people who recognized your value. You began to approach challenges with **clarity and confidence**, knowing that you could take charge of your own destiny and lead those around you.

The leadership you cultivated wasn't about control, but about **creating direction**—leading yourself and your relationships with integrity, wisdom, and a clear vision of where you wanted to go. The way you communicate, how you handle obstacles, and the presence you bring to any room all reflect the internal strength you've developed.

Seeing Yourself as the Prize

Ultimately, this journey is about recognizing that **you are the prize**—not in a way that's arrogant or egotistical, but in a way that's deeply rooted in your understanding of **your intrinsic worth**. The man you've become is not someone who chases or seeks validation; he's someone who knows his value, holds strong to his principles, and **invites the right people and experiences into his life**.

You are no longer defined by past failures, mistakes, or insecurities. You've broken free from limiting beliefs, discarded the stories that once held you back, and embraced a new narrative—a narrative where you are the creator of your own destiny, and your strength comes from within.

The Power of the Journey

As you look back on the steps you've taken, remember that this journey is ongoing. Growth doesn't have a finish line. **Strength** is a continual practice, a way of life, and a daily commitment to **being better** than yesterday. The most powerful men are those who never stop evolving—who continue to refine themselves, learn from their experiences, and rise above their challenges.

You are a work in progress, and that's what makes you powerful. But understand this: you have already achieved so much in transforming from **weakness to strength**. The man you are today is a testament to your dedication, courage, and commitment to becoming your best self. And with this foundation, there's no limit to what you can achieve—whether in your relationships, your personal life, or your career.

The Final Step: Own Your Power

As you conclude this journey, don't see it as the end. Instead, think of it as the beginning of an even greater chapter—one where you **own your power**, **embrace your masculinity**, and continue to walk through life with strength, clarity, and purpose. The world is yours to conquer, and the best version of yourself is always one decision away.

You are the prize—not just in the eyes of others, but in your own eyes. And that's the most empowering realization of all.

The Dating Game is a Mirror of Self

One of the most powerful realizations in the realm of dating and relationships is that the dating game is, in many ways, a mirror of yourself. Every interaction, every connection, and every person you meet is a reflection of the energy you bring to the table. The way you approach dating reveals more about your internal world than you might realize. If you're struggling with attracting the right kind of person, it might be time to reflect on the deeper, often subconscious patterns you are projecting.

Dating isn't just about finding someone to share your life with—it's about **understanding yourself** more clearly and recognizing where you may still have work to do on your own growth. This section will explore how the dating process reflects your own inner world and why embracing this mirror can be one of the most transformative tools in your journey toward attracting high-value relationships.

What You Attract Reflects Who You Are

When you're navigating the world of dating, it's easy to fall into the trap of thinking that the people you meet are random or disconnected from your own behavior. But the reality is that the types of people you attract often align with your current mindset, self-worth, and emotional state.

If you find yourself continually attracting **disempowered, needy, or emotionally unavailable people**, it's likely a reflection of your own **insecurities, lack of boundaries**, or emotional **unavailability**. Likewise, if you often find yourself in relationships where you're constantly giving, sacrificing, or being taken for granted, it may reflect an internal belief that you're **not worthy of being treated with the respect and care you deserve**.

On the flip side, when you've built your own self-worth, emotional maturity, and healthy boundaries, you'll naturally attract people who resonate with that energy. You'll find that the people who come into your life are more **aligned with your values**, **supportive of your growth**, and able to offer you the same level of respect and commitment that you give them.

In this way, dating becomes less about "finding the right one" and more about **becoming the right one**—the version of yourself who is aligned with the type of partner you desire. It's not that the universe is conspiring to send you tests; it's that **your external reality reflects your internal beliefs and energy**.

The Mirror of Expectations

The expectations you have for a partner also reveal a lot about who you are and what you value in yourself. If you have unrealistic standards or constantly find yourself disappointed by others, it's worth questioning whether these expectations are **rooted in your own unmet needs** or **unresolved personal issues**. For instance, if you are overly focused on external traits—like looks or status—you may be neglecting the deeper qualities that are necessary for building a lasting connection, such as **emotional intelligence, respect, and shared values**.

Equally, if you're too eager to please or compromise to keep someone interested, it could signal an underlying fear of rejection or a lack of confidence in your own worth. Relationships based on these types of dynamics will rarely lead to fulfilment because they are built on **a fragile foundation** of **external validation** rather than mutual respect and trust.

Dating, at its core, is an opportunity to understand what you truly **value in yourself** and what you are looking for in a partner. When your **expectations align with your self-worth**, you'll notice that the people you encounter reflect those standards back to you. You'll no longer feel the need to settle for less than you deserve, and instead, will begin to attract individuals who reflect your growth, confidence, and vision for the future.

Dating and Personal Growth

Dating is not just a game of matching with the right person—it's a journey of **personal growth and self-discovery**. Every date, every interaction, and every connection is an opportunity to learn something new about yourself. Are you afraid of rejection? Do you struggle to be vulnerable? Are you terrified of being judged? These fears and patterns often come up in the dating game, and each instance serves as an opportunity for you to explore and break through your own barriers.

By viewing dating as a mirror of your own development, you can begin to see the areas where you still need to grow. Perhaps you realize that you struggle with being present on dates, or maybe you notice a tendency to overthink or become anxious. Instead of seeing these moments as failures or reasons to give up, embrace them as clues. They show you where you can **shift your mindset**, **improve your emotional intelligence**, and build stronger self-confidence.

For example, if you find yourself withdrawing from emotional intimacy, it may be a reflection of your fear of being hurt or rejected. By **addressing these fears directly**—through self-reflection, therapy, or journaling—you are likely to find that you become more open, authentic, and ready for a deeper, more fulfilling connection with a partner.

The Mirror of Boundaries

One of the most significant areas where dating acts as a mirror is in the reflection of your **boundaries**. Your ability to set and enforce healthy boundaries is crucial not only in your relationships with others but in how you treat yourself. If you constantly overstep your own boundaries to accommodate someone else's needs or desires, you are sending a signal that you don't prioritize your own well-being. This will often attract people who have **disrespectful or demanding** tendencies.

On the other hand, if you are firm, clear, and respectful about your boundaries, you'll attract people who honor them and engage with you in a way that respects your autonomy. Strong boundaries also help you avoid falling into unhealthy dynamics, such as **co-dependency**, **people-pleasing**, or **emotional manipulation**.

By setting boundaries that reflect your self-respect and values, you are not only teaching others how to treat you, but you're also reinforcing your own sense of **personal power**. Dating becomes less about pleasing others and more about finding someone who aligns with who you are and respects the life you've created for yourself.

Final Thoughts: The Power of Self-Reflection

Ultimately, the dating game isn't about external validation—it's about **self-reflection**. When you view dating as a mirror, you begin to see every interaction, every date, and every relationship as an opportunity to deepen your self-awareness and align more closely with who you truly are. It's an ongoing process of learning, evolving, and becoming more in tune with your needs, desires, and boundaries.

The more you understand and embrace your own growth, the more you'll attract people who are also on a path of self-discovery, self-improvement, and mutual respect. And as you continue to become the best version of yourself, you'll not only transform your dating life—you'll transform your entire approach to relationships.

Stay Mission-Driven, Not Woman-Driven

One of the most common traps men fall into in dating and relationships is becoming **woman-driven**—allowing their focus, energy, and sense of identity to be governed by the women in their lives. While it's natural to want to connect deeply with someone you care about, when you make a woman the center of your world, you risk losing your sense of self and your purpose. Instead, the most powerful, grounded men in relationships are those who remain **mission-driven**, prioritizing their personal goals, growth, and purpose above all else.

Let's explore what it means to stay mission-driven, why it's essential for your long-term success and fulfilment, and how to apply this mindset to dating and relationships.

The Power of a Clear Mission

When you are mission-driven, you have a clear purpose that drives every aspect of your life. Your mission isn't defined by external validation or approval; it's something you've created based on your values, goals, and vision for the future. Whether it's **building a career**, **developing your physical health**, **pursuing your passions**, or **cultivating your inner growth**, your mission is the core of your life. It's the anchor that keeps you grounded, focused, and moving forward.

This mission becomes your **north star**, guiding you through challenges, temptations, and distractions. It doesn't mean that relationships or women aren't important, but they exist **within the framework of your larger purpose**. A strong mission ensures that you don't lose yourself in the pursuit of others' approval or try to shape your life around someone else's desires. Instead, you continue to evolve as the best version of yourself, with a woman being a powerful addition to your journey—not the center of it.

Why Staying Mission-Driven Makes You More Attractive

Ironically, the more **mission-driven** you are, the more attractive you become. Women are drawn to men who have a sense of direction, purpose, and passion. When your life is centered around a mission—something larger than any one person or relationship—it signals strength, confidence, and independence. It shows that you are a man who **has his own life** and doesn't rely on a relationship to complete him.

This independent energy is magnetic because it communicates that you are not desperate for validation or approval. You are already complete in yourself. You have your own **goals**, **interests**, and **boundaries**, which makes you less likely to bend to pressure or compromise on your values. This is incredibly attractive to high-value women who respect your autonomy and want to be with someone who can **add value** to their own life, rather than someone who is dependent on them for emotional or social fulfilment.

When you are not overly focused on a woman, you will find that **you naturally draw her in** with your confidence, direction, and the energy you bring to the table. Women, at a deep level, respect a man who is committed to his mission and is not easily swayed by fleeting emotions or external circumstances. **This type of energy sets you apart from the majority of men** who lose themselves in the pursuit of affection or validation.

The Pitfalls of Being Woman-Driven

The problem with being woman-driven is that it puts the woman at the center of your universe, shifting the balance of power in the relationship. When you prioritize her needs, opinions, and desires over your own mission, you start to **lose your sense of self**. You may find yourself changing your plans, compromising on your values, or ignoring your own goals just to keep her happy. While compromise is necessary in any relationship, **the key is balance**. You should never compromise your **core mission** for the sake of someone else.

Being woman-driven can also lead to **neediness and desperation**, as you begin to shape your world around her rather than creating your own path. This desperation not only diminishes your value in her eyes but can also create an unhealthy dynamic where you become overly reliant on her approval. Relationships founded on neediness are rarely fulfilling and often lead to **resentment** and **loss of attraction**.

How to Stay Mission-Driven

1. **Clarify Your Mission**

    If you don't already have a clear mission, take the time to define it. What do you want to achieve in your life? What drives you? This could be a career goal, a personal development aim, a passion project, or a broader purpose in life. When you clearly define your mission, it gives you a sense of direction that you can constantly check back with, ensuring that you are always moving toward something meaningful.

2. **Put Your Mission First**

   Every time you make a decision, ask yourself: Does this align with my mission? Does it serve my greater purpose? Being mission-driven means you don't drop everything for short-term pleasures or distractions. It doesn't mean you never prioritize your partner; it means you keep the long-term vision for your life at the forefront and make choices accordingly.

3. **Stay Focused on Your Personal Growth**

   No matter what stage of dating or a relationship you're in, remember that your **growth never stops**. If your mission is to become a better man in all areas of life, keep investing in yourself—whether that's through learning new skills, improving your physical health, or developing emotional intelligence. When you are constantly evolving, you attract others who are also committed to growth.

4. **Maintain Healthy Boundaries**

   Being mission-driven means that you protect your time and energy. If someone—whether a woman or anyone else—expects you to deviate from your mission or values, you need to be able to set clear boundaries. This is a form of self-respect that keeps you from being pulled in multiple directions. You should always protect your mission as a priority, which will, in turn, make you more attractive to those who respect and value you.

5. **Don't Let Your Relationship Define You**

   A woman can enhance your life, but she should never define your worth or purpose. Your identity and self-respect should come from within, not from the relationship itself. Stay rooted in the understanding that your worth is inherent, not conditional upon anyone's approval.

Final Thoughts: The Strength of Staying Mission-Driven

Being mission-driven is about maintaining a **sense of direction** and **personal power**. It allows you to stay grounded and centered in your own life while building a relationship based on mutual respect, attraction, and growth. When you remain focused on your mission, you are not only more likely to attract high-value women who resonate with your purpose, but you are also building a life that is fulfilling and meaningful for you—whether or not you're in a relationship.

When you are woman-driven, you run the risk of losing yourself. But when you are **mission-driven**, you ensure that you remain strong, independent, and confident—a man who knows where he's going, what he stands for, and how to create the life he desires. And that, above all else, is the most attractive quality you can bring into any relationship.

Keep Evolving – The Work is Never Over

In the journey of self-mastery and attracting high-value women, one of the most important truths to understand is that **the work is never over**. Personal growth is not a destination; it's an ongoing process—a journey, not a finality. Many men fall into the trap of thinking that once they've made certain improvements or reached certain goals, they've "made it" and can relax. But the most successful and fulfilled individuals, particularly in relationships, are those who embrace the fact that **growth is continuous** and they are always evolving.

This section will explore why continuous evolution is essential for long-term success, both in dating and in life, and why the work you put into yourself is never truly finished.

The Illusion of "Arriving"

In a culture that loves quick fixes, it's easy to fall into the trap of thinking that achieving a certain level of success or making progress in your life means you've arrived. You've reached the pinnacle of confidence, physical fitness, wealth, or dating success. But the truth is, **there's no finish line**. Once you achieve one

199

goal, you'll set another. Once you improve one area of your life, there's always another that requires attention.

For example, you might have worked hard to build your physical health and strength, but maintaining it requires ongoing effort. You may have reached a level of success in your career, but you'll need to continue evolving to stay competitive and fulfilled. Relationships require constant maintenance—communication, emotional growth, and learning to navigate the complexities of long-term connection.

Personal growth, in every area of your life, is like a muscle—it needs to be constantly worked and stretched. **The illusion of arriving** can be dangerous because it leads to complacency. **If you stop evolving**, you stagnate, and when you stagnate, you begin to lose the very qualities that attracted the people and experiences you want in the first place.

Why Continuous Growth is Key

1. **Increased Self-Awareness**

    As you grow, you begin to develop a deeper understanding of yourself. You become more aware of your strengths, weaknesses, triggers, and desires. This self-awareness allows you to make more conscious choices in your life and relationships. It also enables you to handle challenges with wisdom and clarity because you understand your own tendencies and how to navigate them.

2. **Attraction Through Personal Evolution**

    The more you evolve, the more you have to offer in your relationships—whether romantic, familial, or social. When you continue to develop, you naturally become more **attractive**, not only in terms of your appearance, but in your energy, mindset, and ability to bring value to those around you. People are drawn to those who are always growing, because it signals that they are **capable of handling change**, embracing challenges, and pushing past their limits.

3. **Building Emotional Intelligence**

    As you evolve emotionally, you build the capacity to understand and navigate your own feelings and those of others. This allows you to communicate better, resolve conflicts with ease, and create deeper, more fulfilling connections. Emotional intelligence is a key ingredient for long-term success in relationships because it helps you stay grounded, even in the face of difficult emotions or challenging situations.

4. **Adapting to New Challenges**

    Life, dating, and relationships are filled with new challenges—whether it's navigating the complexities of a relationship, adapting to career changes, or growing through personal hardships. As you continue to evolve, you develop the resilience and problem-solving skills needed to handle these obstacles effectively.

    The growth you do today prepares you for the challenges you will face tomorrow, allowing you to handle them with greater ease and confidence. It's like building a muscle that will allow you to tackle whatever life throws your way, without losing your sense of balance or purpose.

5. **Avoiding Complacency and Entitlement**

    When you stop evolving, you start to believe that the world owes you something—that your past achievements should be enough to carry you forward. Complacency is dangerous because it breeds entitlement and a sense of **passivity**. The truth is, the world doesn't owe you anything, and people are constantly looking for the next version of themselves, whether in personal growth or relationships. **If you stop growing**, the world moves on without you, leaving you in the dust of your past accomplishments.

    The key to long-term success is to never stop evolving. The moment you begin to rest on your laurels is the moment you begin to slip into stagnation.

Practical Ways to Keep Evolving

1. **Invest in Continuous Learning**

   Growth doesn't just happen on its own. It requires **intention**. Make a commitment to yourself to keep learning, whether that's through books, courses, mentorship, or personal development seminars. Learning is the foundation of evolution—it keeps your mind sharp and your perspective fresh.

2. **Set New Goals and Challenges**

   Always have something you're striving for. As you hit milestones, don't stop and bask in the glory—set new, more challenging goals. This keeps your energy and drive alive. Whether it's pushing yourself physically in the gym, mastering a new skill, or setting a new financial target, **always raise the bar**.

3. **Develop Self-Reflection Practices**

   Take time to reflect on your progress, your behavior, and your mindset. Journaling, meditation, and self-reflection allow you to gain insights into where you're growing and where you still need work. This introspection is crucial for making adjustments and continuing your growth.

4. **Challenge Yourself Outside of Your Comfort Zone**

   The greatest growth happens when you step outside of what's familiar and comfortable. Take risks, try new experiences, and **embrace discomfort**. Whether it's traveling to a new place, having an uncomfortable conversation, or trying something you've never done before, **embracing discomfort** forces you to evolve and adapt.

5. **Surround Yourself with Growth-Oriented People**

   The people you spend time with can either **inspire or limit** your growth. Surround yourself with those who challenge you, encourage your progress, and hold you accountable for your ambitions. **Healthy, growth-minded relationships** elevate you and keep you focused on continuous improvement.

Final Thoughts: The Never-Ending Journey

Keep evolving because there's always more to discover about yourself. You will face new challenges, new stages in life, and new opportunities to grow. There will always be areas of yourself that need work—whether it's emotional, physical, intellectual, or relational. The key is to embrace that the work never truly ends and that each step you take forward compounds, building a stronger, more evolved version of yourself.

Embrace the journey and let go of the idea that there's an "end" to your personal development. **The greatest gift you can give yourself is to commit to lifelong growth**—because the more you grow, the more you'll be able to give to others, including the women who walk alongside you in your life.

The work is never over. And that's exactly why the journey is worth taking.

The High-Value Man Creates, Leads and Attracts

To be a truly high-value man is not just about achieving a set of external goals or accumulating status—it's about embodying a mindset and a way of life that **creates value** in every area of your life. The high-value man is someone who **doesn't wait for opportunities** to come to him; he **creates** them. He doesn't follow the crowd; he **leads** with purpose, vision, and integrity. He doesn't simply attract people, things, and relationships into his life; he **magnetizes** them with his presence, energy, and commitment to excellence.

In this section, we'll break down how the high-value man creates, leads, and attracts—key principles that will set you apart and elevate every aspect of your life.

Creating: Mastering the Art of Value Creation

At the core of being a high-value man is the ability to **create value**—whether that's in your personal life, your career, or your relationships. **Creation** is the foundation of progress. A high-value man doesn't sit back and wait for success or fulfilment to come to him. He actively participates in **building his future**.

1. **Creating Opportunities**

    The high-value man doesn't simply react to the world around him. He actively **creates opportunities** for himself. He doesn't wait for the perfect job offer or the right moment to start a new venture; he goes out and **creates his own path**. Whether it's building a business, developing a new skill, or expanding his network, the high-value man understands that success comes from **initiative**. He seeks out opportunities and creates the conditions for his dreams to flourish.

2. **Creating Impact**

    High-value men are not just focused on achieving personal success—they want to **leave a lasting impact**. Whether through their work, their passions, or their relationships, they are driven to create something meaningful. They approach life with the mindset that every action they take should add **value** to the world and to the people around them. When a high-value man creates, he does so with purpose and intention. His work, his ideas, his energy, and his leadership leave a **positive imprint** that extends beyond himself.

3. **Creating Fulfilment**

    True value creation also involves creating a life that fulfills you. High-value men take the time to **design their lives with intention**, understanding that personal satisfaction doesn't come from external accolades or accomplishments alone—it comes from the internal alignment of who they are and what they're doing. By focusing on growth, purpose, and integrity, the high-value man creates a life that brings him deep fulfilment. And from this place of fulfilment, he is able to **serve others** and contribute in powerful ways.

Leading: The Power of Purpose and Vision

A high-value man is also a **leader**—not just in the traditional sense of managing people, but in how he leads his own life and influences others. Leadership is about **direction**—having a sense of purpose and the ability to inspire and motivate others.

1. **Leading by Example**

   The high-value man leads through action. He shows others how to live with integrity, purpose, and discipline. Rather than simply telling others what to do, he **embodies the values he promotes**. Whether it's his work ethic, his physical fitness, his emotional intelligence, or his relationships, the high-value man sets a standard that others naturally gravitate toward. He leads by example, creating an environment that encourages others to strive for excellence, just as he does.

2. **Taking Responsibility**

   True leadership begins with taking full responsibility for one's own life. A high-value man doesn't blame external circumstances, people, or luck for his success or failures. He understands that his life is **a result of his own decisions and actions**, and he takes ownership of that. He doesn't passively drift along with life's currents—he **takes the helm** and steers his own ship. This sense of responsibility extends to relationships and leadership roles. He leads with the understanding that his choices shape not only his future but also the lives of those around him.

3. **Leading with Vision**

   Vision is what fuels the high-value man's drive. He is always looking toward the **future**—where he is going, what he wants to achieve, and how he can contribute to the world. This vision is what keeps him focused, determined, and clear about his priorities. When a man has a compelling vision, it **inspires those around him** to support and follow him. Vision gives him the clarity to make decisions and the energy to keep moving forward, even in the face of obstacles.

Attracting: Magnetic Presence and the Power of Authenticity

While creation and leadership are essential elements of a high-value man's life, the third cornerstone is **attraction**. Attraction, in this sense, isn't just about romantic or sexual appeal—although that certainly plays a role. It's about being someone who naturally attracts **respect, admiration, and opportunities** because of the energy, authenticity, and integrity you bring to the world.

1. **Attracting by Being a Man of Substance**

    High-value men attract not by being flashy or seeking attention, but by cultivating **substance** in their lives. They are interesting, dynamic, and deeply committed to their own growth. When you become a man who **lives with purpose**, who actively creates, leads, and grows, you don't have to chase or force attraction—it naturally flows toward you. The attraction comes from **being the best version of yourself**, from mastering the inner game of self-worth, confidence, and value.

2. **Attracting by Maintaining Integrity**

    The most powerful form of attraction is **authenticity**. High-value men do not pretend to be something they're not in order to gain approval or attract others. They are real, transparent, and true to themselves. This authenticity builds deep trust and connection, and it is the ultimate form of magnetism. People are drawn to those who are confident enough to be **themselves**, unafraid of judgment or external validation. When you embrace your true self, you **attract people who appreciate you for who you really are**, not for a persona you've created.

3. **Attracting by Mastering Emotional Intelligence**

    The high-value man understands the **importance of emotional intelligence** in creating meaningful relationships. He attracts people not by manipulation, games, or tactics, but by being in tune with his emotions and those of others. He is **compassionate, self-aware, and able to navigate the complexities of human interaction** with ease. His emotional stability and maturity make him a safe, reliable presence in any relationship, whether personal, professional, or romantic.

Final Thoughts: The Power of Creation, Leadership, and Attraction

To be a high-value man means to **create, lead, and attract** in every area of your life. You don't wait for life to hand you success—you **create it** through your actions, mindset, and values. You don't follow others—you **lead** with purpose, vision, and integrity, influencing those around you with your example. And you don't chase people or validation—you **attract** others through your authenticity, emotional intelligence, and the power of your presence.

When you embody these qualities, you don't have to fight for what you want in life—it comes to you, naturally and effortlessly. **The high-value man is magnetic, powerful, and fulfilled**, because he understands that true success is not about external possessions or superficial appearances. It's about creating the life you want, leading others by example, and attracting the respect, love, and opportunities that come from living with purpose.

www.ingramcontent.com/pod-product-compliance
Lightning Source LLC
Chambersburg PA
CBHW021144130626
46554CB00005B/1657